PROGRESS THROUGH MENTAL PRAYER

Printing Statement:

Due to the very old age and scarcity of this book,
many of the pages may be hard to read due to the
blurring of the original text, possible missing pages,
missing text and other issues beyond our control.

Because this is such an important and rare work, we
believe it is best to reproduce this book regardless of
its original condition.

Thank you for your understanding.

PROGRESS THROUGH
MENTAL PRAYER

BY

REV. EDWARD LEEN
C.S.Sp., M.A., D.D.

NEW YORK
SHEED & WARD

NIHIL OBSTAT: INNOCENTIUS APAP, S.TH.M., O.P.

CENSOR DEPUTATUS

IMPRIMATUR: JOSEPH BUTT

VIC. GEN.

WESTMONASTERII, DIE, 27^a. IULII, 1935.

FOREWORD

THE instructions on prayer given to the public in these pages are meant to be a help for the ordinary soul. They are printed at the request of very many who are kind in stating that they have found them helpful to themselves. May they prove of use to others, inspire them with an ambition to cultivate an interior life and bring them into close friendship with Jesus Christ. It may appear rash to publish a work on prayer and the spiritual life. It is a Saint's field. The saints and others have written amply, beautifully and in a way that cannot be equalled of these matters in which they were personally so versed. Why then, publish another work on this subject on which so many valuable treatises already exist? The answer is an old one. God can, and does, make use of the most imperfect and, in themselves, useless instruments. It is quite possible, then, that He, in His boundless power and goodness, may make use of this little work for the good of souls. If even one soul is benefited and drawn nearer to God, the labour spent in the writing of these pages, will have received ample compensation.

EDWARD LEEN.

Senior Scholasticatte
of the Holy Ghost Fathers.
Blackrock,
Dublin.

CONTENTS

PART I

THE NATURE OF PRAYER

vii

PART II

METHOD IN MENTAL PRAYER CONSIDERED IN ITS FUNDAMENTAL PRINCIPLES

PART III

ELEMENTS THAT MAKE FOR PROGRESS IN MENTAL PRAYER

INTRODUCTION

INTRODUCTION

SAINT PAUL, writing to the Christian converts, addresses them as persons called to be Saints. It is clear from this mode of address that, in the eyes of the Apostle, the vocation of every Christian, as such, is that he be a saint. To the Apostle's mind this calling, once one has been baptised, is ineluctable. To evade it to the end is not merely to risk but actually to incur everlasting unhappiness. Startling as this thought is, there is not needed much reflection to see that its truth cannot be gainsaid. Nothing " unsaintly " can find place in heaven. What is definitely and by irrevocable choice " unsaintly " is for ever excluded from the presence of God, and this is necessarily so by the very nature of things. It is not in consequence of a stern, arbitrary and, if He chose, revocable decree of banishment issued by God that the unholy soul is banned from heaven. The unholy soul simply could not exist in heaven. It would shrivel up in a veritable agony. It could no more exist there than could a dry twig in a blazing furnace. Light is not more incompatible with darkness than the sanctity of God with what is unholy. It is the infinite purity, the perfect sanctity of God that makes heaven impossible for the unsaintly. Since eternal happiness depends on sanctity, it is important to have a very clear notion of what it consists in and of the way by which it is attained.

What is sanctity? The philosophers, aiming at making clear what a thing is, very often prepare the way by pointing out what it is not. This procedure is a great help towards the acquisition of clear ideas, and can be applied in the present enquiry with some advantage. By very many sanctity would very probably be defined as that which renders a person eligible for canonisation. Such a definition would be too exacting. Those who are placed on the roll of honour of the Church and are offered to the veneration and admiration of the faithful are heroic saints. The process of canonisation reveals the elements of heroic, not of ordinary, sanctity. In an army it is not only those decorated with the official insignia of valour who are good, brave and trustworthy soldiers. In God's army the official saints are the specially distinguished. There are multitudes of others who make good the vocation of which the Apostle speaks and verify in their lives the notion of Christian holiness. Therefore sanctity is not to be limited to heroic sanctity.

Neither may sanctity be confounded with ethical perfection. One cannot be a saint without having all the qualities that go to make a man, but those moral perfections that constitute the perfect ethical man[1] do not constitute the saint. One might, abstractly speaking, possess and practise all the moral virtues, prudence, justice, temperance, fortitude, and all the others that come under these heads— one might realise the ideal of the perfect man traced by the moral philosophers and yet not be a saint.

Christian sanctity is a supernatural thing. To know what it is, recourse must be had to the eternal source of the supernatural, namely, to God Himself. God

---

[1] By ' ethical man ' is meant the man who possesses all the natural virtues in perfection without grace. Needless to say that in the present order this is purely an abstract idea.

is the supreme Saint. Holy is His Name.[2] He is Sanctity Itself, and therefore the exemplar and prototype of all sanctity. The holiness that is not modelled on His is not veritable holiness. Hence it was that Jesus said to the multitudes: "Be ye therefore perfect, as also your heavenly Father is perfect".[3] It is as if He said, "You must be saints, and if a man is to be a Saint, he must be like God".

In what does God's Infinite Holiness consist? It consists in His Infinite Charity, that is in His Infinite love of Himself. This statement needs a little explanation and expansion for, as it stands, it might appear to the superficial to savour of an immense egoism.[4] God is Holy, not for the reason that He loves Himself but because That which He does love with an infinite intensity is what merits to be infinitely loved and chosen for its lovableness. God Himself embraces in Himself all that verifies the notions of Good.[5] He loves that Infinite Good infinitely and in that lies His Infinite Holiness. He loves proportionately every created participation of that all-complete Good. He loves these created reflections of the Infinite Good,

[2] Cf. Isaias vi. 3. And they [the seraphim] cried to one another and said: Holy, Holy, Holy, the Lord God of hosts.

[3] St. Matt. v. 48. cf. Levit. xi. 44. "For I am the Lord your God. Be holy because I am holy."

[4] Egoism is disordered love of self. God's love of Himself is not disordered, since He loves in Himself that Divine Goodness which merits to be infinitely loved and is the reason why anything else is worthy of love in any degree. Theologians speaking of God's love of Himself call it ' most pure love ', to signify that it cannot be tainted by the disorder of egoism. When, in full submission to the Divine Will, we labour to realise in ourselves the designs which God has for us, we may be truly said to love ourselves. Neither is this love egoism, for it is an ordered love—we love ourselves, as it were, in God. But when we seek to gratify ourselves independently of God, when our self love does not spring from (and is not nurtured by) the true love of God, then we are guilty of egoism.

[5] This means that (in scholastic language) the formal reason of God's

not for themselves, but as being ectypes of that which
is the object of His Infinite complacency. In that lies
His Holiness and He loves Himself in these things.

For men and angels also, sanctity lies in the love
of that which is worthy of most supreme love. It
is synonymous with the love of God, and is measured
by that love. It is scarcely necessary to remark that
this love of God is not a sentiment, a feeling, or an
emotion. It is of the will, not of sensibility.[6] It consists
in a deliberate election, choice and preference of the
Supreme and Infinite Good, above all else. God,
the Infinite Good, as revealed by faith, is made the
supreme object of desire to the rejection of the claims
of all other good things that can be selected in His
stead and substituted for Him as an object to which
the will should adhere. This adherence of the will
to God is nothing else but the conformity of the human
will with the Divine; man wills the same things as
God wills; he rejoices in what pleases God and is
saddened by what displeases Him; he does God's holy
Will with all care and accepts from His hands the
daily cross. This total surrender to and conformity
with the Divine Will implies that the Soul has willingly
yielded to the attractiveness of God, and this willing

---

holiness is that He loves infinitely what is worthy of being infinitely loved.
Concretely that which He does love is Himself, therefore it is only materially
speaking (to use a scholastic expression) that God is holy because He loves
Himself.

[6] Too often the word 'love' is associated exclusively with the emotional
movements that accompany natural affection. This is a mistake. True love,
even though it be natural, is not in the emotions but in the will, and the
emotional movements that often accompany it must not be mistaken for it,
nor are they necessary for its existence. St. Thomas gives the true notion
of love when he says that 'to love is to will that good should befall a person';
" amare est velle bonum ". If all this is true of natural love, with how much
more force can it be applied to love that is supernatural.

yielding is love. That man is a Saint for whom the attraction of God is supreme above all other attractions. To be a Saint is to be effectively enamoured of the beauty of God, to desire Him and to desire nothing which would conflict with that desire of God. As for God Himself, so also for man, the love of the Supreme Good carries with it a love of every created participation of that Infinite Good. But that created good must not be loved for itself. It must be cherished because it is of God, and because its beauty is a reflection of His.

Amongst these created participations of the Infinite Good which is God, one of the fairest is the supernatural perfection of a rational creature. God made man to be man. He made him to be something more. By the infusion of Sanctifying Grace He made him to be a being whose moral excellence should be touched with divinity. The man of God's design in the actual order of things is one whose soul should be equipped not only with the moral but also with the theological virtues. The human participant of the Infinite Good is one in whom exists Prudence, Justice, Fortitude, Temperance, along with Faith, Hope and Charity. The state of soul realised by the possession of these seven virtues is good and an object of desire. Aiming at sanctity means aiming at a life in which all these virtues are steadily and constantly operative.

Jesus Christ was the man who realised this ideal in all its perfection. He was, in a supreme measure, prudent, just, brave and temperate. Instead of Faith and Hope He possessed from the first their consummation in Vision.[7] In charity, that is ardent love of God, the Infinite Good, He could not be rivalled. In Him, human perfection, as planned by God, was fully and perfectly realised. God could look upon this handiwork of His Divine Spirit and say that 'it was Good'. As such, it was an object, a thing, loveable and to be desired. Jesus could, and did, love His own moral and spiritual perfection. But He did not make it an object of desire for its own sake. It was God that He loved in this perfect earthly mirror of God's Beauty. If He wrought in His life and in His actions such a perfect masterpiece of moral and spiritual excellence, it was not for the sake of, or because He was drawn by the attraction of that moral excellence in itself. He did it because it was God's Will that He should do so. God's will is identical with Himself. To seek God's will perfectly in all things is the same as to pursue the Supreme Good in all things. This Jesus did. He did not exercise virtue for virtue's sake, but because he apprehended it as God's will. Through and in the act of virtue He as man kept united with God, His Supreme Good.

The spiritual life is sometimes spoken of as the seeking after perfection. If this be understood to mean that the man aiming at spirituality is to set before him *his own*

---

[7] Faith and Hope are virtues belonging to the state of the wayfarer. In our celestial Fatherland, belief will have found its perfection in knowledge, Hope will have passed into possession. But because Charity unites us to God even in this life, its perfection in the next is not something specifically different but is a closer and more intense union with the divinity : " Charity never passeth away."

As regards the Beatific Vision, Christ was never a wayfarer; He enjoyed the sight of God from the moment His human soul sprang into existence. Faith and Hope then He could not have, for He already possessed something more perfect. But His Charity was most intense.

perfection as an object after which he is to strive, it is apt to lead to serious mistakes in the spiritual struggle. It is true that the development of a full spiritual life involves in its attainment man's perfection; yet it is not precisely at this perfection that he must aim, but at God. God is the final end of man and therefore the object after which he must strain in all his spiritual and moral endeavours. The spiritual life may be more clearly, simply and correctly described as the " cultivation of intimacy with God " and the following pages are an attempt to show how, ordinarily speaking, the soul may cultivate that intimacy, and how it is to overcome the obstacles it encounters in its efforts to become intimate with its Creator. God has smoothed the path for the human soul by becoming man. To become intimate with God, the soul has only to become intimate with Jesus, who is like to the soul in his humanity, like to it in all things except sin.[8] Man can grow in friendship with God by growing in friendship with One Who is a fellow-man. The spiritual life is the process of growth in charity, that is in love of Jesus, true man and yet true God. This love not only binds the soul to Jesus, but has the intrinsic effect of assimilating it to Him, transforming it to His likeness. " But he who is joined to the Lord," writes St. Paul, " is one Spirit."[9]

It is to be observed that the Saviour in tracing for men the path they were to tread in order to enter into this union with Him, did not point to Himself saying, " Behold in me the pattern of, and the living object lesson in every human virtue, prudence, justice, courage

[8] Heb. iv. 15.　　[9] 1 Cor. vi. 17.

kindliness, truth and the rest". He did not say,
" Seek to acquire all these virtues which you see in
their perfection in me and then you will become my
intimate friends ". His instruction was much more
direct and simple. He said, " Learn of Me, that I am
meek and humble of heart ".[10] One has only to be
humble after the model of Jesus and all else will follow.
How this is so is not immediately apparent ; for the
full implications of the virtue of humility are not readily
seized. Elsewhere a full analysis of this virtue will
be given. What is there said may be summarily
expressed thus. Humility consists in making God all
and oneself nothing in one's life. [It is, to use a phrase
expressive, but perhaps, of unfortunate associations].
" God over all." It is the practical acceptance of St.
Michael's battle cry : Quis ut Deus ! Who is like
unto God ! It is the complete obliteration of all the
false claims of self, in face of the all pervading sovereignty
of God. All that is required on the part of the Christian
to make perfect his calling, is to efface himself before
God. Hence it is that the whole burden of the Saviour's
teaching to men is the practice of self-abnegation.
Self-abnegation is something much larger than either
suffering or mortification. The instructions on prayer
that follow are an exposition of the mode by which
this conquest of self is carried to a final and successful
issue. Prayer, properly carried out, will have as its
effect the gradual revelation to the soul of this disease
of self-love which so intimately penetrates the very
fibres of its being as to pass unobserved by the person
that does not lead an interior life. In prayer the soul

[10] St. Matt. xi. 29.

gradually draws into the radiant purity and truth of the soul of Jesus. It becomes bathed in and penetrated through and through with that radiance; and in this splendour all in it that is of self and not of God, all that is in it unlike Jesus, stands clearly revealed to that soul's own gaze. When this unlikeness is purged away by the action of suffering and the sacrament of the Eucharist, then the close union of the soul with God takes place.

Prayer, mortification and silence prepare the soul for the action of the Blessed Eucharist. Once the obstacles are cleared away from the soul this great Sacrament of union accomplishes in its perfection that which is its special effect, namely the creation of a union of spirit between the soul and Jesus. Prayer prepares the way for this, for prayer that is good must have as its effect the gradual growth in self-abnegation. The presence of self-love in the soul is the great obstacle to the action of grace. Prayer reveals the presence of this self-love and secures the aid of God to its extermination. The grace of Jesus flowing to the soul through prayer and the Sacraments carries out this process of extermination. As the Christian soul empties of self, it fills up with God, not merely with some thought or aspect of God as visualised by a self-centred spirituality or even as revealed in created reflections, but with God as He is in Himself and as He reveals Himself to " little ones". To be filled with God is to be perfect with the very perfection of our heavenly Father, but this happy result is conditioned by the soul's practical application of the means explicitly stated by Our Divine Guide and Exemplar : " Learn of Me that I am meek and humble of heart".[11] It is in no narrow or particular sense that God is said " to resist the proud and to give grace to the humble ".[12]

In these words of the Apostle is revealed the connection, not logically immediate, between humility and spiritual perfection. Humility is not fortitude nor temperance nor yet charity. But where it exists all these will exist. For the Christian supernatural virtues, the only ones that avail for union with God in this life and in the next, are not acquired but infused. God gives them. They are communicated with grace. They grow with grace and are proportioned in their perfection to the measure of grace. God gives grace generously to the humble. To each He gives according to the measure He has predestined, which is not the same for all. But each one in his own individual case receives according as he is more or less perfectly disposed to receive. As humility is perfect so is the disposition perfect. The perfectly humble man will flourish in all virtues. He will be fearless, temperate, kind, loving, and all the rest. He has not to accomplish acts of temperance to have the virtue of temperance. He has it already in virtue of grace and in a strength proportioned to that grace. The acts merely give a greater facility in the exercise of the virtue and dispose the soul for a further increase of grace. So it is in the case of each of the other cardinal virtues and in the case of the Theological Virtues.

It is sad that of all those who start out with such confidence and such goodwill on the supernatural life, so very few attain to any marked degree of spiritual-

[11] St. Matt. xi. 29.   [12] St. James iv. 6. cf. 1 St. Peter v. 5.

ity. The causes of this very general failure are known only to God. They are necessarily inscrutable to us from whom are hidden the secret resistances of the created will. Resistance to grace is the reason of the absence of growth in the spiritual life. Yet it would be hard to say that the resistance is in the majority of cases deliberate. It is quite possible that it may proceed from want of spiritual enlightenment, and that great numbers of failures are to be attributed not to bad will but to an imperfect understanding. It is quite possible that souls do not succeed simply because they employ faulty methods or make a faulty use of good ones. Self-knowledge is needed for growth in the spiritual life. St. Catherine of Siena stresses this point with great emphasis in her writings. Now perhaps the concentration of the soul's attention on the constituent elements of the virtues that it ambitions to attain and of the vices it longs to eradicate may impede the growth of self-knowledge. One who has some experience in dealing with souls cannot fail to remark that very many good and promising beginnings end in disappointment and discouragement. Such a one will observe that generally speaking—not absolutely speaking—there is a common cause for this. It is due to the soul's being continually occupied by the symptoms of its spiritual state, be these symptoms healthy or the reverse. Its gaze ranges over the whole field of the virtues and the whole field of the vices and it brings its own daily conduct into relation with these. It aims at development by striving after the practices of the virtues and by eliminating theactivities of the vices. In this it can fail to go to the radical cause of its growth or rather of its absence of growth in virtue.[13] An example from medicine will make this clear. When a patient presents himself to a doctor and reveals that he is suffering several kinds of pain and in different parts of his body there are two courses of action open to the medical man. He may deal with each form of suffering and by the resources of his skill bring alleviation to one after the other. In due time the patient is discharged from the hospital free from suffering, but only to fall back into his old state in a short time. If he has found a very skilled doctor his experience will be different. The expert physician will set himself to find out in his patient the " focus of infection ", which is the source of the various ills the sufferer complains of. If this ' focus ' is discovered and eliminated the patient leaves hospital not temporarily but permanently cured. In the spiritual world there is an unerring and divine Physician. It is Christ Himself. He has diagnosed the " focus of infection " in every soul. It is " self " in its varying forms and manifestations. Eliminate this and there ensues necessarily a healthy spiritual life. Hence it is that He preaches self-abnegation in the first place, He preaches it in the second place : He preaches it all the time. On it all depends. Self-abnegation is but humility in act : it is the practical carrying out in action of the precepts of that fundamental virtue.

Jesus is the perfect type of humility of soul : He is the perfect model of self-abnegation in act. Mental prayer is the means by which the soul grows into the spirit of Jesus, developing in itself " the mind of Christ ".

[13] It seems to me from practical experience that this is very often the case.

If the soul that practises mental prayer does not grow in humility and self-abnegation it is a sign that its prayer is badly made and is not fulfilling its purpose. It is essential for spiritual progress that one should have a clear vision of the rôle that prayer has to play in this progress. That rôle is the development, through loving contemplation of the Man-God, of the fundamental dispositions of the Sacred Humanity. Little by little the soul grows in that basic humility so characteristic of Christ; complete dependence on and loving subjection to God become as it were the leaven which spreading by imperceptible degrees pervades its every action; it is marked by a self-abnegation which aims at purging from it everything that is not God, so that "conformed to the image of His Son" it may live its life in full accord with the designs of Providence in its regard.

PART I

THE NATURE OF PRAYER

" *Let nothing hinder thee from praying always, and be not afraid to be justified even unto death : for the reward of God continueth for ever. Before prayer prepare thy soul : and be not as a man that tempteth God.*"

Ecclesiasticus xviii. 22–23.

PART I

THE NATURE OF PRAYER

CHAPTER I

THE AIM OF MENTAL PRAYER

*" My thoughts are not your thoughts, nor your
ways my ways, saith the Lord."* Isaias lv. 8.

THE science of prayer is the science of the
intercourse of man with God. Prayer itself
is the unfolding of our mind before the most
High and in His presence. It begins by a desire on
the part of the soul to put itself in the presence of its
Creator; in its development it tends to become an
interchange of thought and affection between the soul
and God. This unfolding of our mind before the
Almighty is not an idle and egoistic self-analysis. It
is the exposition of one's sentiments, needs and
aspirations. It is prompted by a desire that God should
supply the soul's needs: it is sustained by the firm
confidence that God is disposed to give the soul all
that the soul is created to obtain from God the Author
of its being.

The *ultimate end* of the relationship established
between the soul and God in prayer, is, that the soul
should, by His help, abandon its own natural earthly
way of thinking and willing, and enter into God's
views and affections, judge things as God judges them.
and therefore conform its thoughts and desires to the

thoughts and desires of God. This conformity of thought and affection between God and the soul, is effected by the soul's conformity in thoughts and affections with Jesus Christ, the God-Man. There is a significance in the injunction of St. Paul: " For let this mind be in you, which was also in Christ Jesus ".[1] The final end of prayer, considered as a potent means for the development of God's life in the soul, is to emancipate us from natural habits of thought and affection and elevate us to a supernatural manner of thinking and willing, to change our natural outlook on life and things and to make it supernatural. The function of prayer therefore (and especially of mental prayer)[2] is to transform our minds and through the transformation of our minds to effect a change in our dispositions and in our hearts. This mental conversion is not as simple as it is usually taken to be ; normally it does not take place in a day or in a year ; it involves a process which demands a long time for its completion.

It is not generally realised to what an extent our modes of thought—even when we are leading christian lives—are alien to the modes of thought of God. To think " christianly " is not an easy matter. God warns us of this through the Prophet Isaias : " For my thoughts are not your thoughts, nor your ways my ways, saith the Lord. For as the heavens are exalted above the earth, so are my ways exalted above your ways, and

---

[1] Phil. ii. 5.

[2] Prayer is mental when the thoughts and affections of the soul are not expressed in a previously determined formula. All prayer ought to participate to some extent in the nature of mental prayer because acts of mind and will are always necessary. The ideas touched on in this paragraph are developed in *The Dialogue of St. Catherine of Siena*, Vol. I, chap. xxxvi. (Ed. Hurtaud).

my thoughts above your thoughts ".[3] Prayer aims at
bridging over this infinite gulf; it aims at enabling
us to enter into the mind of God and from that point
of vantage to contemplate all created things and the
mysteries of Faith. To arrive at this view of reality,
it is necessary that it be not the spirit of human wisdom
or prudence that should shed light upon the objects
of our thought, or should reveal what are to be the
worthy objects of affection. It is needful that the light
of merely human understanding be replaced by the
illumination of the Spirit of God. For " the things
also that are of God no man knoweth, but the spirit
of God. Now we have received not the spirit of this
world, but the spirit that is of God : that we may know
the things that are given us from God. . . . But
the sensual man perceiveth not these things that are
of the spirit of God ; for it is foolishness to him, and
he cannot understand because it is spiritually examined.
But the spiritual man judgeth all things. . . . For
who hath known the mind of the Lord that he may
instruct him ? But we have the mind of Christ ".[4]
To the extent that we remain insensible to the promptings
of the Spirit of God within us, to the degree in which
we have failed to come under the influence of the Divine
communication by God of Himself to us, to that extent
we are what the apostle calls " sensual ". At the beginning
of our " conversion " we are almost entirely " sensual "
in our ways of judging and understanding ; we are
unable to probe the inner meaning and penetrate to
the spirit of the mysteries of our faith. We hold them
as true ; our knowledge is a knowledge of " possession "

[3] Isaias lv. 8-9.   [4] 1 Cor. ii. 11-16.

and not of " use ". These mysteries remain, in a sense, external to us. We know that they are true. Their outward features—that is, the formulae in which they are expressed—are familiar to us, but we have little apprehension of their inner meaning ; hence they exercise little or no power on the affections of our heart or on the direction of our lives. For us the vital meanings pent up like life-giving waters within these formulae and containing in themselves the power to transform and transfigure our human life, have not broken loose and flooded our souls with their refreshing streams. The habit of prayer, and that alone, can correct all this, for it makes us cease to judge sensually and enables us to acquire the art of judging all things spiritually.[5]

The concluding words of St. Paul in the text cited above, namely, " we have the mind of Christ ", perfectly express the result aimed at by the process of mental prayer. In all the varied forms which our intercourse with God necessarily assumes, the desire to acquire

[5] The religious state of the average soul at the beginning of its conversion and prior to its initiation into the interior life, is aptly set forth in the following passage from Newman. " In our condition as average Christians . . . we know that God's service is perfect freedom, not a servitude, but this it is in the case of those who have long served Him ; at first it is a kind of servitude, it is a task till our likings and tastes come to be in union with those which God has sanctioned . . . ' The servant knoweth not what his lord doth ' (John xv. 15). The servant is not in his lord's confidence, does not understand what he is aiming at, or why he commands this and forbids that. . . . Such is the state of those who begin religious obedience. They do not see anything come of their devotional or penitential exercises, nor do they take pleasure in them ; they are obliged to defer to God's word simply because it is His word. . . . We must begin religion with what looks like a form. Our fault will be, not in beginning it as a form, but in continuing as a form. *It is our duty to be ever striving and praying to enter into the real spirit of our services, and in proportion as we understand them, they will cease to be a form and a task and will be the real expression of our minds. Thus shall we be gradually changed in heart from servants into sons of Almighty God."* Parochial Sermons. Vol. iii. Sermon 7.

this mentality, the mentality of Jesus Christ, must act as a guiding and unifying principle.

We cannot flatter ourselves to have made any *considerable* progress in prayer until we have advanced in learning to think with God—understanding Him and His ways. We cannot be *properly* intimate with Him until this has taken place. The reason is obvious for one who studies ordinary human relationships. How constrained and artificial and laboured are our conversations with those with whom we have little in common ! How difficult it is to find satisfaction in the company of those who are completely out of sympathy with our attitude towards life ! How often it is the lot of Catholics to meet with non-catholics— who are equipped with the ordinary human virtues, men who are fair minded, upright and trustworthy but who have no clear perception or understanding of the supernatural. A sincere Catholic, no matter how kindly disposed, will inevitably find intimacy with such persons extremely difficult if not impossible. No matter what apparent agreement there may be in many minor points there is really little or no common ground of understanding. This difficulty is intensified infinitely in our relations with God. Prayer is an intercourse or communing of the soul with God according to the words of St. Paul :—" Our conversation is in heaven ; from whence we look for the Saviour, our Lord Jesus Christ, who will reform the body of our lowness, made like to the body of His glory, according to the operation whereby he is able to subdue all things unto himself ".[8] " In my opinion," says

[8] Phil. iii. 20-21.

St. Teresa, " prayer is only a friendly intercourse in which the soul converses alone with Him by Whom she knows she is loved."[7]

Now this personal intercourse cannot exist, or can exist but very imperfectly unless there is some common ground of understanding—some identity of thought and interests. For it must be remembered that, according to St. Thomas, prayer is an act of the reason, that is to say, it must have a basis in the intelligence. Growth in prayer is merely a growth in familiarity with God.[8]

In all prayer there are two agents to be considered. There can be no converse with God unless the soul wants it and actually enters on it, and the soul cannot desire to pray or actually engage in prayer unless God is at hand. God is the principal agent, prompting the first desire of the soul for intercourse with Him; His Holy Spirit influences the intellect, awakens pious thoughts in the memory, arouses the imagination to develop and preserve these thoughts, draws the reason to examine religious truths and excites holy desires conformable to the thoughts He has inspired. Desiring more intensely to communicate Himself to the soul, than it could desire union with Him, He directs every effort it makes in its intercourse with Him. God's

[7] *Life.* Ch. viii. St. Thomas quoting St. John Damascene, says that prayer is an ascent or an approach of the mind to God. ii. ii. Q.83. a.17, ad 2. St. Gregory Nazianzen says that prayer is a conference or conversation of the soul with God. *De. Or. Dom.* I. According to St. John Chrysostom it is a discoursing with the Divine Majesty. *Hom.* 30 *in Gen.* St. Augustine speaks of it as an affectionate turning of the mind to God. *Serm.* ix. 3.

[8] (*a*) The conformity or harmony of will between the soul and God is a conformity of the human will as enlightened by reason and faith. It does not exclude an actual opposition to the Divine on the part of men's lower or sensitive nature. (*b*) St. Thomas says the function of friendship with God is to bring about that men should incline to the same things as God. He quotes with approval Aristotle, saying: "One of the features of friendship is that friends should have a liking for and choose the same things ".

action does not exclude that of the soul. Diligent co-operation on its part is vitally necessary; the soul must petition God for the grace of prayer, and at the same time spare no pains to conform its thoughts and ways to those of God.

A very touching and intensely human incident in the Gospel illustrates all this, and carries us rapidly through the various stages of the intercourse of the soul with God, from its initial want of comprehension to the final illumination by which its ignorance of the divine is swept away. As the evening of the first Easter day was drawing to its close, two of the followers of Jesus of Nazareth left Jerusalem and directed their steps towards a small town about eight miles distant, called Emmaus. As was natural, their thoughts revolved around the tragic happenings of the previous days. Seeing nothing in these sad events but the frustration of all their hopes and the end of their ambitious dreams, they were plunged in gloom. Their state of mind is well portrayed in their own words : " but we hoped that it was He that should have redeemed Israel : and now besides all this, to-day is the third day since these things were done ".[9] Yet being unable to tear their thoughts away from what they had witnessed, they could speak of nothing else.

As they walked and talked, a stranger drew near, and being anxious to interchange their thoughts with another, they were glad when he came to share their company. " And it came to pass that while they talked and reasoned with themselves, Jesus Himself also, drawing near, went with them." [10] The disciples being

[9] St. Luke xxiv. 21.   [10] St. Luke xxiv. 15.

asked by their new companion what it was that was
the subject of their conversation, expressed surprise
at any one being ignorant of the terrible scenes which
Jerusalem had just witnessed. " And he said to them :
what are these discourses that you hold one with another
as you walk and are sad ? And one of them, whose
name was Cleophas, answering, said to him : art thou
only a stranger in Jerusalem, and hast not known the
things that have been done there in these days ? "[11]
The stranger asked them to explain what they referred
to, and straight away both proceeded to sketch the life
of Him Whose followers they had been. He was a
great prophet, mighty in word and work ; they had
expected great things of Him, for on His remarkable
power they had based their hopes of the restoration
and the freedom of Israel. And now all had ended
in disillusionment and tragedy. The mighty worker
of wonders was seized without difficulty by the priests
and princes, and put to death without opposition.
All was over. " And they said : concerning Jesus of
Nazareth who was a prophet, mighty in word and
work before God and all the people ; and how our
chief priests and princes delivered Him to be condemned
to death and crucified Him : but we hoped that it was
He that should have redeemed Israel."[12] It was true
that some women asserted that He had arisen again
from the dead, but that was a tale that had its origin in
the overwrought imaginations of women, distracted
by the cruel sufferings and death of the Jesus whom
they loved. " Yea, and certain women also of our
company affrighted us, who before it was light were

[11] St. Luke xxiv. 17–18.   [12] St. Luke xxiv. 19, 20, 21.

at the sepulchre, and not finding His Body, came saying that they had also seen a vision of angels, who say that he is alive."[13]

This story of the resurrection the disciples were not prepared to admit. It conflicted with their sense of what should be the normal development of the events of the three years that had just ended. Evasion of death they expected, but a death and resurrection did not fit into their habits of thought. Regarding Jesus, His life, His work and His life's purpose from a viewpoint that was to a large extent natural, and interpreting it from that viewpoint, they completely misjudged the life and misunderstood the Man. Their appreciation of the events of the last days of Holy Week, showed that they had never properly understood Him Whom they called their Lord and Master.

The stranger after having allowed them to express themselves fully on the subject that filled their thoughts, and having listened to them in silence to the end, began to speak in his turn. " Then He said to them : O foolish and slow of heart to believe in all things which the prophets have spoken. Ought not Christ to have suffered these things, and so to enter into His glory ? "[14] Taking their minds back over the Scriptures, He set before them contemplation after contemplation on the life, the character, the disposition and the sufferings of the Messias. As feature after feature was drawn for them, from the words of Moses and the Prophets, especially the great Isaias, they began to see, in the career of Him Whom they had followed, the fulfilment of each detail of the prophecies. At the same time they

[13] St. Luke xxiv. 22, 23.   [14] St. Luke xxiv. 25, 26.

began to understand Jesus of Nazareth and grasp the inner meaning, the lesson, the purpose, of His life on earth. It became clear to them that His was not a life of purely human limitations. The Divine element in it began to show through for them. " And beginning at Moses and all the Prophets, he expounded to them in all the Scriptures the things that were concerning him."[15]

At length it began to dawn upon them that the Redemption they looked for was to be sought not without but within—not in the emancipation of their persons from a political yoke, but in a subjection of their souls to the deifying influence of the Redeemer. As the true portrait of the Messias developed for them under the skilful hand of the Master Himself, their minds grew in understanding of, and their hearts began to glow with love of Him Whom they had so misunderstood. " Was not our heart," they said afterwards to one another, " burning within us, whilst He spoke in the way and opened to us the Scriptures ? "[16]

This walk and conversation with Jesus was mental prayer in its ordinary form. As will be seen further on, it sets before us vividly, if only in outline, the ordinary process through which the soul passes, as it grows in knowledge of Jesus. In considering this Scriptural illustration we should note that: (a) Jesus Himself drew near and went with them; (b) He led them to expose their thoughts and sentiments; (c) He was ingenious in facilitating intercourse and intimacy —*He took the initiative.* In a word, He was the quiet,

[15] St. Luke xxiv. 27.   [16] St. Luke xxiv. 32.

powerful Master of the whole situation just as He is in prayer, if only the soul responds to His advances.

In the beginning the soul, attracted to Jesus by some impulse of grace, comes to Him, filled with natural thoughts and aspirations, and very ignorant of the supernatural. It understands neither God nor itself. It has few intimate relations with the Divinity outside of itself and within itself; but it begins to converse with Jesus. If it persists in the frequentation of His company the Lord gradually takes an ever-increasing share in the conversation, and begins to enlighten the soul. In its contemplation of the mysteries of faith, He aids it to penetrate beneath the words and facts and symbols, hitherto known but superficially, and to grasp the inner sense of the supernatural truths contained in these facts or words or symbols. The Scriptures are gradually opened to the soul. The well-known texts begin to acquire a new and deeper meaning. Familiar expressions convey a knowledge which the soul wonders never to have before discovered in them. All this new light is directed towards giving a fuller and more perfect comprehension of the mysteries of our faith, which are the mysteries of the life of Jesus. From this comprehension springs a love and sympathy with our Divine Lord. There is a growing desire for identification with Him. Union of thought and feeling begets intimacy and constant intercourse; the soul has a constant desire of conversing with Jesus about His interests and its own, which love has made identical. " Consider how great the happiness given to you," says St. John Chrysostom, " how wonderful the glory

bestowed on you, in this that you can discourse to
God, hold conversation with Christ, aspire after what
you are inclined to, and ask for what is wanting to you."[17]
The soul cannot consort with Jesus without ardently
desiring to be like Him, and to liberate itself from whatever can place an obstacle to the freedom of their
mutual relations. It conceives a distaste for all that
tends to create in itself an unlikeness to Jesus. The
constant and habitual aspiration of the soul, running
as an undercurrent through all its communications
with the Lord, is, to be freed from the shackles of all
deliberate faults, even the very least, and to be filled
with grace. "All our prayers," says St. Thomas,
"ought to be directed to the obtaining of grace and
glory."[18]

The soul, striving after this conformity with Him
who has become its Friend, necessarily seeks to enter
into and to develop in itself the fundamental and guiding
disposition of that Friend's soul. That disposition is
the disposition of sacrifice, or rather, a profound
adoration of God finding its expression in sacrifice.
The fundamental disposition of Christ's soul was one
of absolute and loving subjection to God. Jesus Himself expressed this, saying: "For I do always the
things that please Him".[19] Prayer is a means to the
acquisition and cultivation of the spirit of sacrifice of
Jesus Christ. Now, when God finds this disposition

[17] "Considera quanta est tibi concessa felicitas, quanta gloria attributa,
orationibus fabulari cum Deo, cum Christo miscere colloquia, optare quod
velis, quod desideras postulare." St. Chrysostom quoted by St. Thomas,
II. II. Q.83. a.2, 3.
[18] "Quia omnes orationes nostrae ordinari debent ad gratiam et gloriam
consequendam." St. Th. II. II. Q.83. a.4 c.
[19] "Quae placita sunt ei facio semper." St. John viii. 29.

in the soul, He hastens to communicate to it a participation more and more abundant of that Divine life of which the soul of Jesus is a limitless ocean. Thus is realised the purpose of Christ's Incarnation: "I am come", He said, "that they may have life, and have it more abundantly".[20] To the reception of this life all prayer must be directed; "this chiefly we must seek in prayer", says St. Thomas, "namely, to be united to God".[21]

The ascension of the soul then, is, through prayer to the acquisition of the spirit of sacrifice, and thence to union with God especially through the Holy Communion. "The Blessed Eucharist", says Cardinal Billot, "is the chief means that God has ordained for imparting the divine life to the soul. That outpouring of divine life is proportioned to the dispositions of the soul that receives it. The more perfectly the soul has entered into the dispositions of Jesus, the more closely it has become akin to Him in taste and outlook, the more abundant is the reception of the divine life that in its plenitude resides in Jesus."[22] Prayer, Spirit of Jesus developed by mental prayer, Communion— that is the order. This is perfectly exemplified in the incident cited from the Gospel. At first the disciples failed to recognise Jesus. After conversation with Him their faith was purified, their devotion to Him grew, and they at length understood and entered into the meaning and spirit of His life and Passion. He saith to them: " O foolish and slow of heart to believe

[20] St. John x. 10.
[21] " Quia hoc praecipue est in oratione petendum ut Deo uniamur." St. Th. II. II. Q.83. 2.1, ad 2.
[22] *De Ecclesiae Sacramentis.* Vol. I, p. 94. Editio quinta.

in all things which the prophets have spoken. Ought
not Christ to have suffered these things and so enter
into His glory?"[23]   And then they understood and
accepted the principle of sacrifice for Him and for
themselves, as the sole means to that redemption which
is of the soul, not of the body. They had dreamed of
a redemption that was wholly political and external,
one which changed their worldly status, leaving themselves unchanged. Now they understood redemption
as something wholly internal and spiritual, liberating
them from the yoke of their own fallen nature and
giving their souls the regal condition of the sonship
of God. The imparting of grace, not the bestowal
of earthly position, they now understood to be the
object of Christ's relations with them. But the end
was not yet. All this was a preparation for
something further. "And it came to pass whilst
he was at table with them, He took bread, and
blessed and brake, and gave to them. And their
eyes were opened and they knew Him."[24] With
the reception of the sacred Host, came an inflow
of Divine grace into their souls and their final
illumination.

Having sketched in outline the nature and aim of
prayer in its fundamental character, it remains to point
out the different forms which it takes, to show that
growth in the habit of prayer is the same as the
development in spirituality, to expose the usual
temptations and difficulties which the soul experiences
in the cultivation of the interior life, to describe
the route which progress in this life follows, to

[23] St. Luke xxiv. 25–26.   [24] St. Luke xxiv. 30–31.

explain the ordinary mechanism (if the word be permitted) by which the intercourse with God is maintained, and finally to disclose the obstacles that impede, as well as the conditions that help advancement.

CHAPTER II

*" My heart hath said to Thee, I have sought Thy
face. Thy face, O Lord I will seek."* Ps. xxvi. 7.

WITHOUT prayer salvation is impossible. To
neglect it is to neglect the only means given
us to remain in touch with Almighty God;
if we lose hold of Him we necessarily fall back upon
ourselves, and in ourselves we can find nothing that
can advance us towards eternal life. Everything that
appertains to that must come to us from God. Every
gift in the supernatural order is an effect of His bounty,
" for every best gift and every perfect gift is from above,
coming down from the Father of lights ".[1] God has
ordained that these gifts be given to us on condition
of our valuing them, desiring them and petitioning
Him humbly for them. He says to us: " Ask and
you shall receive ". This implies—" if you do not ask
you shall not receive ". We do not beg except for
what we prize highly and are desirous of possessing.
There is no true prayer where there is not a real longing
for the things pertaining to the development of the
spiritual life. All that tends to impart, to strengthen,
to develop and perfect that life, are the gifts which God
is prepared to give the soul, if the soul nourishes in itself
a holy desire for them, acknowledges its need of them,
and confesses its dependence on God for them.

The most necessary resolution for one that wishes
to draw near to God and to grow in intimacy with

[1] St. James i. 17.

34

Him, the resolution that embraces and involves all the others, is that of persevering in prayer in spite of all the difficulties and trials to be met with in it.[2] For though it is true that prayer is supernatural, " for no man can say the Lord Jesus, but by the Holy Ghost ",[3] still the habit of prayer is fixed and strengthened and developed in much the same way as natural habits are formed and developed in us. It depends, therefore, for its firmness and force on our own diligence, knowledge and industry, aided of course as is always to be understood, by the grace of God.

It is an entirely mistaken notion to think that the gift of prayer is something which in no wise depends upon us, but is altogether God-given. Prayer, it is to be emphatically stated, does not ' happen ' to us ; we do not ' contract ' spirituality as people contract a disease—by accident. Such a view fosters spiritual sloth, by which the soul excuses itself for not entering into relations with God on the grounds that it feels no taste of inclination towards such intercourse and waits until God imparts this devotional taste before beginning.

Again it is certain that the power to pray is a grace ; but this grace is infallibly given if we on our side fulfil the conditions required of us. Our co-operation is necessary. We must not wait until influenced by pious sentiments or emotions, or driven by necessity

[2] Cf. *Dialogue of St. Catherine of Siena.* God the Father speaking to the Saint says : " Know, my daughter, that it is by persevering in prayer that is humble, incessant and full of faith, that all the virtues are acquired by the soul. It ought, then, to persevere and never to allow itself to be forced to give up, either by the illusions of the devil or by its own frailty, that is, by the thoughts that harass it, nor by the restlessness of the body, nor by the idle talk that the devil puts in the mouths of men, to turn the soul from prayer."

[3] 1 Cor. xiii. 3. cf. Ss. Theol. II. II. Q.83. a. 13. c.

to address ourselves to God. These pious feelings are
not of the essence of prayer. We must be so trained
in the exercise of the divine converse, that we can
approach God with as much constancy when we feel
a positive distaste for the supernatural as when carried
away by an access of sensible devotion. We must
learn to speak to God independently of our tastes and
feelings. The difficulty in prayer is not in prayer itself.
It all comes from our want of decision in electing
definitely to find our unique satisfaction of mind, will
and imagination in the supernatural and in definitely
renouncing the tendency to seek in the natural world
any form of satisfaction that does not lead to God.
If we are strong enough and resolute enough to choose
God as the term not of some, but of all our activity,
if we are resolute enough not to be continually oscillating
between Him and creatures, prayer is easy. As regards
petition, there is no difficulty in asking for what we
like.[4] The whole world is daily occupied in that.
Most deputations are concerned with it. It is the
characteristic action of childhood. But there is a real
difficulty in liking what we, as children of God, should
ask for. Naturally we have no taste for the things
of the spiritual life. It is intelligible that we should
be very half-hearted in our petitions for what we do not
strongly desire. We are not prone to be very insistent
in our demands for what we are not very eager to have.
Of course, Christians as a rule are not conscious of
this distaste for the supernatural. They sincerely

---

[4] Prayer of Petition is prayer in the most restricted and precise sense.
St. Thomas referring to petition says : " Prayer is a certain manifestation
of the human will ", and again : " Prayer is a certain unfolding of our will
to God that He may fulfil it". III. Q. 21. a. 1.

believe that they are quite earnestly beseeching God for the things of eternal life. There is a certain amount of unconscious self-deception in this matter. The petition for the things of eternal life is accompanied very often, in fact most frequently, by a keen desire of, and longing for things that are an impediment to that life. One desire, of necessity, negatives, at least partially, the other and renders it to some extent illusory. If what is actually longed for is in contradiction with the life of grace or opposed to its development, the prayer for the things of the spirit is but an idle formula, a complete self-delusion. The cherishing in the soul of desires incompatible with the longing for God, is the secret of the vast number of failures in the spiritual life.[5] Of the many that embark on the interior life, few, comparatively, succeed. The reason lies in this, hat they have never resolutely *chosen* God to the rejection of all else beside, or that having once made the choice, they afterwards allow themselves to develop likings that impede or conflict with the growth of God's life in the soul. They allow themselves to drift into choosing other things as well as God. This inevitably tends to not choosing God at all. Many will plead that they find the spiritual life a difficulty, because they find prayer a difficulty. The truth is that men begin to find prayer a difficulty when they have begun to find God a difficulty. This comes when God has ceased to interest them because other things have begun to interest them more.[6] The essential condition

[5] St. John of the Cross develops the importance of mortifying our desires in the *Ascent*, Book I.

[6] Cf. Ss. Th. II. II. Q.35. a. 1 and 2, which articles treat of this state of soul.

of success in the spiritual life is to train oneself " *to want* " God and to school oneself " *not to want* " what does not lead to Him. Hence it is that St. Catherine of Siena in her *Dialogue,* stresses so much the necessity of stirring up and nourishing in the soul this holy desire.[7]

[7] *Dialogue,* Vol. I, chap. 36.

CHAPTER III

" *All ye works of the Lord, bless the Lord.*" Dan. iii. 57.

THERE are two distinct ways in which the soul presents itself before its Creator; that is, there are two distinct types of prayer, namely, vocal and mental. Now, though a mental attention either to the meaning of what we are saying, or to the Person we are addressing, is required, in order that the formulae we utter with our lips merit the name of prayer, there is, nevertheless, a fundamental difference in the nature and the purpose and the effects of these two modes of communicating with God.

The word prayer is derived from the most characteristic act of this exercise, that is, petition. All our dealings with God must have a background of pleading in them; a note of entreaty must run through the varied movements of the soul towards its God. There is always one ultimate object which is aimed at in the converse of men with God, and to this object all others must be subordinated; that is, that God communicate Himself to His creatures in this life as a preparation for union in the next. We are indigent before God; we need everything and He alone can give us what we want. If we had not fallen, our utterances would mainly consist of words of praise and adoration and worship. And though now, as has been said, there is an element of petition always present in our intercourse with God, yet praise, adoration and thanksgiving are still the most characteristic functions of prayer when it is vocal. For this reason it has to be more formal than mental prayer. In the latter the operation is more personal and intimate. In the former, God is the direct object of our acts. In mental prayer we can have our own soul and its states as the object on which will or understanding is exercised. Though people pray vocally in private, yet it is characteristic of, and usual for vocal prayer to be recited in common. Vocal prayer is always to a certain degree a public act, and as such is something that is done to honour and reverence God. Of course prayers in common are often recited, as in times of calamity, to express repentance, to plead for mercy, to placate God's justice or to obtain His blessings. But the distinctive function of vocal prayer remains that of honouring, reverencing and worshipping God.

The most sublime form of vocal prayer is the *Divine Office*. This is formed of language inspired for the most part by the Holy Ghost Himself to give expression to the thoughts that should animate all created supernaturalised intelligences in the presence of the great Lord of all. The ideas contained in the Psalms and the words in which they are clothed are such as man, were he a perfect child of God, would use to give expression to his admiration, love, reverence and esteem for his heavenly Father. The holy Pope Pius X, quoting Saint Augustine, writes: " That God might be praised in a fitting manner by man, God Himself composed the praises of Himself. And because God deigned to praise Himself, man found the terms in which to sound God's praises ".[1] The psalms are, therefore, a divine

[1] *Divino Afflatu.*

composition which God's servants are to repeat in His presence to honour Him. In doing this they stand in a relation to God similar to that of the beatified who ever stand before His throne honouring Him by heavenly canticles. God desires that we should deal with Him much in the same manner as that in which we deal with one another. It is our custom at school, for instance, when we wish to honour a distinguished guest, to have passages from some famous author declaimed, or musical pieces from a great composer performed in the presence of him whom we wish to honour. In a somewhat similar manner the Holy Ghost has inspired for us the praises which we are to recite or chant before God to honour Him.

The nature of public vocal prayer demands that we acquit ourselves of it with great reverence and respect; our every gesture, tone and attitude must be made to signify the honour we wish to pay to the Great Being in whose presence we are. For the merit and perfection of our act it is not demanded that we should necessarily advert to the meaning of the words we use; if the whole action is directed towards God, if we realise that the formulae we use are in themselves eminently pleasing to Him, and if from the beginning we form the intention of acquitting ourselves well of the duty we are undertaking, the whole function is meritorious and pleasing to God whom we honour.[2]

[2] God the Father speaking to St. Catherine of Siena says :—" The soul must not separate vocal from mental prayer; while it pronounces the words, let it strive to lift up its thoughts and direct them towards my love : to this let it unite the consideration, in general, of its faults and of the precious Blood of my Son, in which she may recognise the bountifulness of my charity and the remission of its sins."—*Dialogue:* Vol. I, chap. 36.

Any subsequent distraction or want of attention, as long as it is indeliberate, does not destroy the initial intention. This intention extends its influence over the whole multitude of acts which constitute the service.

The monastic choir is as a stage arranged before the King of heaven—a stage on which those who recite the Divine Office should endeavour to execute with great expression and feeling, attention and perfection, those chants in honour of God, composed by the Divine Spirit. Those who recite the Divine Office should remember their rôle in the divine drama. It is that of the Mystical Body of Jesus Christ, the Church, whose inmost thoughts and feelings, whose mystical life, whose states of soul and whose love and devotion to God the Father, the divine hymns express in terms of wonderful variety and perfection. The Divine Office differs from all other vocal prayers. It is the official utterance of the Spouse of Christ, whose accents exercise an unparalleled influence over the heart of God. "The Church by her faith, her confidence, her love and her union with Jesus, annihilates the distance that separates her from God and chants His praise like the Word in the Bosom of the Trinity. She, united with Christ, sings the very praises of God under the eyes of God." [3]

What has been said of the Divine Office is true in its degree and measure of all vocal prayer. In every

[3] Cf. Marmion. *Christ the Ideal of the Monk.* Chap. xiii, Part iii, p. 299. The public prayer of the Church is in very truth the prayer of Christ. Sharing as we do in His life, forming but one body in Him, we become *His* instruments, by which He can praise God. If we place ourselves wholly at His disposal, it is He who prays in us, with us, by us. Thus we become one in a very full sense with the eternal Praise and glory of His Father.

case there is a recital of a formula, composed nearly always by a person different from him who prays. It does not necessarily express the disposition of soul of the person employing the formula; if it be an approved prayer, it voices sentiments, thoughts and emotions which are in themselves pleasing to God. Of course the more perfectly one identifies oneself with the thoughts expressed in these recited formulae, the higher the value of the prayer. But it is clear from what has been said that in the form of address one stands on a more formal and distant relationship with Almighty God, than in the case of mental prayer.[4]

The effect of vocal prayer upon the soul varies with the stage of development the soul has reached in the spiritual life. For those who do not lead an interior life, the rôle of such prayer is restricted to exciting a sense of the supernatural and a sense of the duty of raising the mind to God; for those advanced in the spiritual life, the liturgical prayers are of a sovereign efficacy for bringing their souls into union with the intellectual illuminations and affective impulses of the Holy Spirit. The prayers and chants of Holy Church become for such souls the natural and spontaneous outlet in which the pent up emotions of the heart acquired in mental prayer find due expression.[5]

[4] A recollected bearing, a reverential attitude and a becoming posture are demanded for the due acquittal of vocal prayer. When vocal prayers are recited in common, the exercise should be marked by something of the decorum and dignity that surrounds the choral recitation of the Divine Office. Such an exercise should always be begun with the express intention that God should receive thereby a due measure of honour and worship.

[5] The soul is turned into the fire of love and therefore every word is like a spark rising from a fire inflaming and enlightening the powers of the soul,

To acquit ourselves perfectly of vocal prayer, it is
necessary to raise to God our mind by attention,
our heart by devotion, and our will by submission.
These dispositions deliberately stirred up in the
soul at the beginning will colour the whole exercise,
in spite of distractions. Actual attention all the
time is not vital. Our prayer is meritorious and
obtains its effect provided we begin with an attention
that is not afterwards retracted by any voluntary
distraction. Of course actual attention the whole
way through is to be aimed at, for it gives additional
force and efficacy to our words[6] We should make
it a point to begin well, by deliberately putting
ourselves in the presence of God, and by withdrawing
our powers from outward things, recollecting them in
ourselves and fixing them on God. If distractions

that she listeth ever to pray and do nothing else. And the body, is an instrument, and a trumpet of the soul in which the soul bloweth sweet notes of
spiritual prayers to God. Hilton. *Scale of Perfection.* C.12.

[6] The words of St. Thomas, marked as usual by clarity as well as wisdom
are to be quoted in this connection. " Now prayer has three effects. The
first is common to all acts informed by Charity, and this is merit. In order
to realise this effect, it is not necessary that prayer should be attentive throughout ; because the vigour of the original *intention* with which one begins
to pray makes the whole prayer meritorious, as is the case with other meritorious acts. The second effect of prayer is proper to it alone, and consists in
impetration : and again the original *intention*, to which God looks chiefly,
suffices to obtain this effect. But if the original *intention* is absent, prayer
lacks both merit and impetration : because as Gregory says (*Moral* xxii.)
' God hears not the prayer of those who have no *intention* of praying '.
The third effect of prayer is one which it produces immediately ; this is the
spiritual refreshment of the mind and for this effect *attention* is a necessary
condition : wherefore St. Paul writes : (1 Cor. xiv. 14) : ' If I pray in a
tongue . . . my understanding is without fruit '.
" It must be noted however that there are three kinds of *attention* that can
be brought to vocal prayer : one which watches the words, lest we say them
wrong, another which attends to the sense of the words, and a third which
aims at the end of prayer, namely, God and to the thing we are praying
for. This last kind of attention is most necessary and even the untutored are
capable of it." (IIa. IIae. Q.83. 2. 13.)

come, we must aim at having all our distractions turn
on Divine things ; this we can do by learning to view
all things in God's light. The power to do so is the
direct effect of the cultivation of the habit of mental
prayer.

CHAPTER IV

THE ORDINARY PROCESS OF MENTAL PRAYER

" I am the way ; no one cometh to the Father but
by Me." John xiv. 6.

MENTAL Prayer is an ascent or approach of
the mind to God. It is nothing else than a
communing of spirit with spirit, a communing
of the created intelligence with the uncreated. To
pray, therefore, it is necessary to be present with God.
When we wish to enter into conversation with our
friends on earth, we leave the place in which we are
and transport ourselves to where they are or make
use of those means of communication invented by
science. No use of a medium of communication or
change of position on our part would seem to be
necessary when it is question of coming into the presence
of God, since He is everywhere, and in Him we live,
move and have our being. Yet, strange to say, though
we are surrounded by, and, as it were, enveloped in
God, still we can fail to have Him present to us. For
a spirit makes other beings to be present to it not by
local movement but by its acts. Our soul has present
to it only those objects about which its faculties are
engaged. We can be said to be present only there,
where our thoughts, affections or imaginings are. It
is in the very same way we are present with God.
We are in God's presence only during the time when
the faculties of our soul are exercised about Him or
His attributes or in something that has a bearing on
our relations with Him. The meaning therefore, of

having placed ourselves in God's presence—of our mind having ascended to Him—is that God has become for us an object of loving, or at least interested, thought. This imports as its correlative aspect, the withdrawal of our imagination and our senses, our will and our intellect, with the acts that flow from them, from all objects other than God.[1]

We are in a real sense present where that object is which occupies our imagination—more truly present where it is than where we may happen to be locally. A familiar illustration may be drawn from a too common experience in a teacher's life. The indifferent and distracted student is bodily present in the class-room, but his surroundings and the teacher's words make no impression on him as he allows his thoughts and interests to wander to the joys of home or the excitement of the playing fields. He is, in a human sense, more present where his thoughts and affections are than where he is in body.

God is a pure spirit—and we are not. We cannot come into His presence as an angel can. All the acts of our intellect depend on the senses and on the imagination. We must have some imaginative image of a thing in order to be able to think on it. It is difficult for us to form an image of the Divinity and therefore difficult for us to be present with God. At least it would be very difficult for us, had not God in His kindness, found a way by which access to Him, by aid of the imagination, might be made easy for men. That way was the Incarnation.

[1] Ven. Libermann, *Ecrits Spirituels*, p. 82. no. 2.

The Divinity is made present visibly and tangibly to us in the Humanity of Our Lord: " That which was from the beginning, which we have heard, which we have seen with our eyes, which we have looked upon, and our hands have handled, of the word of life; for the life was manifested; and we have seen and do bear witness and declare unto you the life eternal, which was with the Father, and hath appeared to us ".[2] Our Lord shadows forth in a visible manner the perfection of God—His goodness, His benignity, His holiness, His mercy. Those attributes in a pure spirit we should have found very difficult to imagine or conceive. As clothed in, and expressing themselves through the Sacred Humanity, these attributes of God are become accessible to human imagination as well as to human thought. Jesus is the spotless mirror of the Divinity. Therefore, the study of the life of Jesus and His works —the contemplation of His humanity—forms the imaginative ground-work from which the soul forms to itself the spiritual concept of God. " Everything in Jesus is not only saintly but sanctifying also, and imprints itself on the souls which apply themselves to the consideration of it, if they do so. with good dispositions. His humility makes us humble; His purity purifies us; His poverty, His patience, His sweetness and His other virtues imprint themselves on those who contemplate them. This may take place without our reflecting at all upon ourselves, but simply by our viewing these virtues in Jesus with esteem, admiration, respect, love and complacency."[3]

[2] 1 John i. 1–2.
[3] Faber. *Bethlehem*, chap. i. Quoted from Rigoleuc *L'Homme d'Oraison.* p. 35.

Hence it is that our communion with God, the presence of our spirit with His, is accomplished through the Sacred Humanity. Therefore, the ordinary way of mental prayer or meditation[4] is the reviewing in our imagination and in our intelligence the life and words of Jesus.

This however is only one part of prayer—it does not end with considerations or reflections, for prayer in its essence is not a mere reflection on a subject belonging to the order of divine things. "It is a supernatural attitude of the soul before its Creator in which it directs itself towards God and unites itself with Him, for the purpose of rendering Him what is due to Him from His creatures, receiving in turn His communications and rendering itself pleasing in His sight."[5] The considerations—that is, the meditation strictly so called—have an ultimate purpose. That purpose is to create in our minds a form or an ideal of life and action, an ideal which is presented by our intelligence to our will, as our highest good. Our considerations, therefore, must tend to form, deepen and strengthen the conviction that the life of the Man-God is the good life for us, that His way of acting and thinking is what is most deserving of our imitation. Meditation has for its object to fill our minds with the conviction that Jesus is the way, the truth, and the life, that is to say, to fill us with the conviction that our life is a false and vain one in so far as it does not conform to the spirit of His; that His values of human things are the

[4] The word " meditation " is used to designate that kind of mental prayer. in which the considerations of the mind are very prominent and prolonged. In this case the name of the first and most salient part is given to the whole.
[5] Ven. Libermann, *Ecrits Spirituels*, p. 294.

only true values; that to attain the goal of existence we must follow the path He has traced and be guided by His principles; and finally, that it is only by making His modes of thought, affection, and action our own that we shall enjoy the life that is truly life.[6] The will necessarily moves with love towards that which the intelligence presents to it as its good. The study of the attractiveness of Jesus creates in the will the desire of conformity with Him and the practice of the virtues exemplified in His life.

There is only one humanity that is united of itself to the Divinity; that is the Humanity of Jesus, for it is united hypostatically. If we are to be united intimately with the Divinity it is necessary for us to prepare the way for that union by becoming assimilated to that Humanity. How is this done? By assimilating ourselves to Jesus in thought, in affections, in principles and in ideals—i.e. by reproducing in our life the features of His human Life. This paves the way for vital union with the Divinity that is in Jesus. This union with the Divinity grows in proportion to the increase of sanctifying grace in the soul. The ordinary channel for the communication of this grace of Christ is the Sacraments. These confer greater or lesser grace as the dispositions of the soul resemble to a greater or lesser degree the dispositions of the soul of Jesus of Nazareth. Therefore our considerations in prayer are meant to set before our will as an object to venerate, to admire, to love and to imitate, the ideal of human life portrayed in the life of Jesus on earth. Our prayer must inspire us with the desire to shape our actions

[6] I Tim. vi. 19.

after the model set up by the Saviour as the means to union with God. We must be attracted to the loveliness of God by the loveliness of Jesus. God is the supreme and ultimate good, and everything else, even virtue, is good only in as much as it leads to the possession of Him.

Of course God reveals Himself to us in the works of creation, and from the contemplation of these, we can acquire a certain knowledge of the greatness, of the power, of the beauty and perfection of God, and with the light of revelation to help we could develop in ourselves a kind of personal regard for the Author of all created things. But this drawing towards God could with difficulty attain to the nature of love; it would remain strongly impregnated with fear and awe: its most perfect expression would be reverence—the reverence of the creature devoted to its Creator. Hence it was that those who lived under the old dispensation scarcely knew God as a Father; for all created things are limited and imperfect, and therefore generate but a very imperfect notion of God; they tend to generate even a false one on account of the weakness of will and intellect that followed on the fall. This was the reason why even the chosen people had such a proneness to idolatry—a thing which many find very difficult to understand. But in our Lord's life the attributes of God are reflected without the slightest shadow of imperfection and in all their lovableness. His sacred Humanity reveals God to us in a most attractive form and it becomes possible for us to love God and desire to be united with Him, this being the end of prayer, as it is the end of all our relations with God.

There can be union only between beings that are alike; to be united with God we must be like Him, assimilated to Him, conformed in the passions and affections of our humanity to the passions and affections of that Humanity which He made His own. That Humanity is the bridge of union between Him and us. The function of mental prayer, then, as an act of our mind, is to study and contemplate the features of the life of Jesus Christ with a view to reproducing the traits of that life in ourselves and so disposing ourselves to growth in the divine life of grace. When we have made progress in this contemplation it is possible for us to fix our gaze on created things, on the world itself and the events that take place in it—and that without danger to ourselves. For the Sacred Humanity has rectified our ideas about all created things and in Its light we can study creatures without fear of being led astray by them. When the mind has attained the view-point of Jesus Christ, distraction in prayer does not normally turn the soul from God, for every object that comes before the mind, every work, every event, is instinctively reviewed in the relation in which it stands to Him, and all will therefore (though at times insensibly) lead the mind back to God.

So far there has been question only of the soul's acts in prayer. These, however, do not constitute the whole of this exercise. Prayer has been defined as a familiar intercourse or conversation with God. It is a being present with God and associating with Him, as we associate with those we love on earth. Now two spirits cannot be present to each other, since such presence is by means of acts, without strongly influencing each other. In this intercourse the activity is not all one sided; it is not wholly on our side. The Divine Spirit is operative as well as the human. God incessantly plays His part and this is an active one. A conversation is not a speech delivered before a person, it involves an interchange of thought; and as our thought is directed towards God, so God's thought is directed towards us.

God is intensely operative and if the soul has willed to draw near to God, He on His side, tends to draw near to it. The effect of the contact of two spirits is one of assimilation, i.e. one is made like the other. The soul by its activity cannot assimilate God to itself, for God cannot change; the activity of God therefore is directed towards assimilating the soul to Himself. God therefore takes up the soul and assimilates it to Himself, and this in proportion as the soul by its own acts, helped by grace, abdicates itself and lives the life of God by acting habitually and intensely under a motive of faith and of charity. When the soul attains to the point of practically always acting not merely under a habitual or virtual, but an actual motive of faith,[7] it has already arrived at an advanced stage in the life of ordinary prayer; for this conscious assumption of all its activities under a rule or principle of faith makes its prayer continuous, uninterrupted and unceasing. The actuality and vividness of the faith clears the soul's activity of the influence of self, and accordingly God's influence enters to an ever higher degree into such activities. Persons who live this

[7] This means an actual intention at the beginning of each small series of acts.

life of faith in a *sustained* manner carry about with them an air of the divine easily perceptible by those with whom they come in contact. There is nothing which helps more to foster and develop this life of faith than the habit of seeing the will of God in all things even the most insignificant, in the petty trials, disappointments, checks and even in the pleasures and satisfactions that come our way.

Thus habitual prayer demands an habitual sense of God's presence—demands, which is more accurate, God being continually present to us. Now there are different and varying degrees of presence of persons, one with another. In a social gathering many people are assembled in the same room within easy reach of one another. All are bodily present in the same place. As is often the case, those who are assembled together in great social gatherings come as strangers one to another. The vast majority of them meet, perhaps, for the first time. What happens is that each looks around in the assembly for the few with whom he is on terms of acquaintanceship or friendship, and engages in conversation with these. For the group thus formed the others are as if they were not there at all. The friends that meet and converse are present to one another; they are present to themselves but not to the others, and this presence deepens in the degree in which their conversation springs from a common interest or causes a deepening of mutual understanding. The more their mutual interests and tastes lead to an active interchange of thoughts and views and to a strengthening of the bonds that bind them together, the deeper grows the

presence. If again one of the guests takes the lead
in the conversation and all the others dominated by
his personality cease to speak and give themselves
to the task of listening, the speaker becomes present
to everybody in the room, but not everybody to him
—those only are present to him who have led him
on to conversation, and interest in whom, incites him
to speak.

So it is, in a measure, in our relations with God.
We have already seen that mere bodily presence before
the tabernacle, or mere recitation of formulae does
not constitute God present to us ; for that, it is needful
that the powers of our soul be occupied with God
and with the things of God. Now in prayer there
is reciprocal action, prayer is a conversation. It is
as essential a part of mental prayer that God should
address Himself to us, as that we should address ourselves to Him.[8] He speaks to us through the deepening
of our faith, through the illumination He supplies
to our intelligence, to the penetration into the mysteries
of our religion that He grants us, and through the
impulse to good that He gives to our wills. He speaks
to us above all, by the life and actions of Jesus Christ
—these are " His Word " to us—His Own " Word ".
" God Who, at sundry times and in divers manners,

[8] St. Francis de Sales says : " Prayer is a colloquy, a discourse or a conversation of the soul with God, by it we speak to God and He again speaks to
us ; we aspire to Him and breathe in Him, and He reciprocally inspires us
and breathes in us ". (Treatise on Love of God, VI.)

St. Vincent de Paul says : " Prayer is a conversation of the soul with
God, an intercourse of the spirit in which God teaches it in an interior way
what it should know and do and in which the soul says to God what He
Himself teaches it to ask for ". (Conf. on Prayer, 1648.)

Abbot Marmion, speaking of prayer says : " In a conversation one both
listens and speaks. The soul gives itself up to God and God communicates
Himself to the soul ". (*Christ the Life of the Soul.* C. x, Part II.)

spoke in times past to the fathers by the prophets, last of all, in these days, hath spoken to us by His Son, Whom He hath appointed Heir of all things, by whom also He made the World, Who being the brightness of His glory, and the figure of His substance, sitteth on the right hand of the majesty on High."[9]

We become present with God by having present in thoughts, affection and in imagination the life of Jesus. We associate with and converse with God by associating and conversing in spirit with Jesus. He Himself said: "Philip, he that seeth me, seeth the Father also."[10] God on His side mingles familiarly with our life and its concerns, through and in the life of His Word on earth. He communicates His light and His Life to us through Him. Jesus is the channel of the communication of divine grace. Prayer consists in living with and conversing with Jesus with a view to becoming like to Him. Prayer is literally the instrument of a transforming process by which we leave our own form and put on the form of The Son of Man. The function of prayer consists in stripping us of earthly desires: "Stripping yourselves of the old man with his deeds, and putting on the new, him who is renewed unto knowledge, according to the image of him that created him."[11] The following words from the autobiography of St. Teresa form a fitting conclusion to the chapter. "By thought we can put ourselves in the presence of Christ, set ourselves gradually aflame by a great love for the Sacred Humanity, keep company with Him at all times, speak to Him, recommend our

[9] Heb. i. 1–3. [10] St. John xiv. 9.
[11] St. Paul, Col. iii. 9–10.

needs to Him, seek compassion from Him in our trials, rejoice with Him in our consolations, keep ourselves from forgetting Him in times of prosperity. Let us not seek to make beautiful speeches to Him; but rather speak simply to express our desires and wants. This is an excellent method and makes us advance in a very short time. The person who studies how to live in this precious company and draws therefrom a genuine love for the Master who has showered so many benefits upon us, that person, I assert, has gone forward in the way of prayer. So that we must not grow disconsolate, as I have already said, if the feeling of devotion is lacking. Let us rather give thanks to Our Lord, Who despite the imperfections in our works, keeps alive within us the desire of pleasing Him.

" This method of prayer, which consists in keeping oneself in the company of the Saviour, is profitable at every stage. It is a very certain means of progressing in the first degree of prayer and of reaching the second in a short time. And in the last stages it serves as a protection against the temptations of the devil."[12]

[12] *Life* by Henelj, Ch. xii.

CHAPTER V

" Let this mind be in you which was also in Christ Jesus."
Philipp. ii. 5.

IN last analysis then, Mental Prayer is the act of the soul seeking the society of Our Divine Lord, with a view to receiving His direction and coming under the control of His Sacred Humanity. His life stands revealed in the Gospel; the soul enters into contact with it, by a loving study of its mysteries. The mother of Jesus has given us the example, she herself passed her life doing what we are called to do. The Sacred writer assures us of this twice, saying, " But Mary kept all these words, pondering them in her heart ",[1] and again he says—" And His Mother kept all these words in her heart ". In Hebrew " word " means " event " or " happening " usually of a striking or mysterious nature. It must not be forgotten that the life and actions of Jesus were mysteries for Mary as they are for us. The meaning of the text, then, is that she reflected on and turned over in her mind the actions and words of her own Child, studying the events of which He was the centre, with a view to probing further into their inexhaustible depths of meaning, in order to be penetrated with the sentiments, emotions and dispositions of Jesus in all these. Mary meditated on the life of Jesus as it unfolded itself before her, exactly as we are asked to do, and for the same purpose—to be steeped in and assimilated to the spirit of that life.

[1] Luke ii. 19 & 51.

58

For meditation on the Mysteries of Jesus is not merely an idle speculation followed by a barren admiration of the truth revealed in the mystery. It must be undertaken with an object in view, namely to become good, avoid vice and grow in virtue as a means to union with God. We practise prayer in order to be assimilated to Our Head and Lord Jesus, to reproduce His life in ours.

When the soul, touched by grace, determines to abandon the routine practice of religion and to cultivate a real interior life, a beginning is ordinarily made by passing from the mechanical recitation of vocal prayers to the practice of Meditation. The first effect of Meditation is to awaken the soul to the realisation that it has a "mentality," an outlook on life, an evaluation of things totally different from that of the Person whose life it has begun to contemplate. This unlikeness in view, in tastes, in tendencies between the soul and Jesus causes the influence of the Saviour to be felt but slightly in the beginning.

We are powerfully moved and affected only by those towards whom we are attracted sympathetically. If we are out of sympathy with a person, it is unlikely that we should be carried away or elevated or inspired to a higher ideal by that person no matter how gifted or virtuous he may be. And it must be confessed that there are comparatively few that have not been at some time of their life out of sympathy with the principles of Jesus and on a very imperfect understanding with Him. Before their conversion men are worldly-minded; and this worldly-mindedness manifests itself in that uneasy feeling they experience when they hear of the maxims of holy men and ascetical writers. The words of the Saints, their appreciation of things, their outlook on life—all is, for worldly men, very chilling and uninspiring. The appeal of humanism is felt to be much warmer. There are few of us in whom these words of Father Faber have not at some time or other found their verification —" There are many who when they hear or read of the spiritual life, or come across the ordinary maxims of Christian perfection, do not understand what is put before them. It is as if some one spoke to them in a foreign language; either the words are without meaning or the ideas are far-fetched and unreal. They stand off from persons who profess to teach such doctrines or live by them, as if they had some contagious disease, which they might catch themselves ".[2]

When a soul fresh from this condition opens intercourse with Jesus, it is obvious that it would be useless for the Lord to speak too much to it. The Lord in His dealings with the soul is interested uniquely in its sanctification. He is not concerned about its earthly prospects except in so far as they have a bearing on spiritual issues. His inner communications to the soul, then, will always have reference to the process of sanctification, and the poor soul, on its side has as yet but little comprehension of what sanctification means and of what its pursuit involves. The soul is therefore not capable of understanding the Lord's intentions unless very imperfectly. But anxious to advance and multiplying its visits to, and its moments of contact with, the Divine Master,

[2] *The Creator and the Creature.* Bk. I, Chap. i.

it begins to enter more and more into the views of its heavenly Director and falls more and more under His influence. At first the soul is in continual activity, the acts that make up the exercise of prayer are practically all its own. It speaks to Our Lord with a dim perception of its wants and a certain realisation of its shortcomings. Acts of petition and contrition form the burden of its communications. The growth of the soul in Divine Grace, that is, in Divine Life, is imperceptible. Yet these pious acts produced by a good will have promoted its development and have imparted a certain amount of spiritual vigour. What is taking place spiritually may be illustrated by the process of bodily nourishment. The sensible, evident part of this process is the introduction of the food into the mouth, its mastication and deglutition. All these operations are capable of observation and control. But it is only when these observed operations are completed that assimilation begins, vitality is imparted and growth promoted. The process which is really life-giving is not an object of consciousness, nor does it fall under observation. In a similar way is it in the beginning of prayer. One is conscious of one's activities of imagination, intellect and will. But there is no perception of the effects that, by the action of grace, follow for the soul on these activities of the faculties. So after the soul has elicited and multiplied its acts, the Lord illumines the intelligence to truth and excites the will to good—in the beginning in an imperceptible way and afterwards perhaps more plainly.

The touches of Divine Grace are very delicate and normally speaking escape our consciousness.

The soul is at the stage when its perceptions of material and natural things is keen, and its perception of spiritual things extremely dull. Still the process of growth in the soul-state, which conditions the supernatural life, goes on. Those acts, that have been spoken of, develop the soul inasmuch as they posit the conditions of development. The development in divine life is of course entirely due to God, the sole source of the supernatural. According as the activity of God on the soul is being exercised in an increasing measure, the soul's own activities diminish. Those of the Lord increase in proportion. The soul simply enters into the Presence of its Director and Guide, who begins to operate powerfully by instructions, illuminations and encouragements. When this arrives at a point where the greater part or almost all the conversation is carried on by the Lord, the soul leaves the ordinary course and enters into the state of mental prayer which is called passive.

Hence we see that mental prayer is active or ordinary and passive or mystical. In the former kind the action of the soul predominates; in the latter, the action of God. When almost the whole activity is God's, the soul has entered into the extraordinary states and has to undergo those fearful purgations which wipe away the last traces of the effects of the original revolt. These purifications remove the final elements of that resistance to the Divine, which is found in our nature since the Fall, and thus God is free (so to speak) to evolve His own life in the soul, and the soul becomes almost powerless to resist the Divine influence.

We make mental prayer therefore, to be converted from evil to good, from good to better, and from better to perfection; its object as has often been stated, is to create in us those conditions of human mind and heart, which are the conditions of the inflow of the Divine into us through the Sacraments; "For let this mind be in you, which was also in Christ Jesus ".[3] The end (to the attainment of which, for adults, mental prayer is an almost indispensable means) is the end of our supernatural being, namely, union with God. Prayer aims at inaugurating that union on earth in the conditions and limitations of mortality. Prayer is not, then, the mere asking of things, but a willing associating with Jesus, in order to pass through Him as man to God—"I am the Way . . . no man cometh to the Father but by me ".[4] The adoption of His principles of life and the application of them to our own life, is the sole way by which we can arrive at that life of which He as man has the plenitude—the Life Divine. A mere intellectual knowledge of the Gospel story does not bring us to this; it is only humble meditation on it, inspired by love, that will bring us to the determination to conform ourselves to the Lord Jesus.

Many give up prayer in disgust because they do not understand its meaning, its nature and its end. They believe prayer consists in asking for graces, spiritual and temporal, the acquisition of virtues or the extirpation of vices, and they pray in the belief that God will bestow virtues just as we make presents of books, or take away our vicious habits as we remove

[3] Phil. ii. 5.   [4] St. John xiv. 6.

dangerous instruments from the hands of children. Virtue is a growth and follows the laws and conditions of growing things; the same is true of vice; in the ordinary ways of Providence the sole mode of its removal is by the growth of the contrary virtue. God does not take away our vices as the surgeon severs a gangrenous limb from the body. We do not get virtues or lose vices merely for the asking. The desire prompting and inspiring our prayer should be the desire of growing in all respects like to Jesus. It is in that growth that vices vanish and virtues make their appearance. We pray to God through Jesus not so much to get something as to become some-thing, namely to become "conformable to the image of His Son".[5] The ultimate object of prayer is to glorify God and we glorify God by being as we should be.

The real end of prayer therefore is to be good, to effect in ourselves the dispositions to sanctification, that is, to purify our souls and replace our natural views by the views of Jesus Christ and to substitute for our natural life, His mode of life. This is done by frequenting the society of Our Lord, by dealing in converse with Him, whatever be the form this converse may take. It may be a seeking for advice and instruction, a communing on common interests, an expression of feeling or sympathy with His sufferings, an exposition of one's own wants and interests, a tribute of praise, admiration or love. The familiar conversation with Jesus may vary very much as to its themes; the effect aimed at must be always a growing conformity

[5] Rom. viii. 29.

to Him. In a word prayer may be considered a going to Jesus for spiritual direction—a direction on the way that is to lead to God. We pray not to dispose God to give, but to prepare ourselves to receive— to receive that plenitude of Divine life which is in Christ Jesus Our Lord.

Note. The brief outline given in this chapter will be developed in the next three.

CHAPTER VI

THE FIRST STAGE IN THE TRANSFORMATION

*" It is written—not on bread alone doth man live,
but on every word that proceedeth from the mouth of
God."* Luke iv. 4.

WHEN the soul moved by grace resolves to
place itself entirely under the direction of
Jesus in view of its spiritual advancement,
it is, ordinarily speaking, full of imperfections. Moreover, it does not realise how imperfect it is. Having
as yet no comprehension of perfection it is without
understanding of imperfection. It is not alive to all
the evil that is active in itself. It comes to Jesus with
a natural outlook, independent, passionate, sensual,
proud, uncharitable, a lover of ease and self-satisfaction.
Novices in the spiritual life are all this, without their
being aware of the fact of anything being wrong with
them in that respect. They know of sin only as a
positive violation of God's Law, and are unaware
that there is an habitual cast of thought, that is more
dangerous than an actual evil act. They come imbued
with the spirit of the world and fashioned to the habits,
formed by the years of living according to that spirit.
Life has been for them a tissue of those ideas, judgments,
sentiments, principles, hopes, fears, desires, regrets
and dreams which envelop the souls of men, corrupt
their vision and little by little hide from them heaven
and the eternity for which they are destined. To
those entering on the spiritual life, things spiritual
have appealed but vaguely, whilst all that can be

seen, weighed, touched and handled, alone have had value in their eyes. The spirit of the world is the spirit which considers life, health, glory, beauty, riches, family, country, goodness itself, without referring them to God their author and end; it looks upon these as objects to possess without any reference to God. Under the influence of this spirit they are attracted to sensible things, to honours, pleasures and satisfactions of all sorts and they are averse from heavenly contemplation.

When God gives the call to the interior life, a ray of Divine Actual Grace penetrates through this darkness that surrounds the soul, revealing to it, in a flash of light, the beauty of the ideal of a spiritual or divine life, and at the same time the will, by an additional grace, is captivated by the beauty of this ideal and moved to embrace it. The soul without as yet understanding anything of the ways of God or of the life of union with Him dimly perceives that it is beautiful and happiness-giving. Then the soul resolves to undertake that search for God which, if persevered in, will end in the finding of Him and of itself.

The beginning of the interior life, is therefore much occupied with intellectual activity. It is devoted to the consideration of what we are, of what God is. It is a study of the Christian life, its principles and its maxims. The will's activity consists in the endeavour to establish in ourselves the conviction that there should be a necessary connection between the doctrine of the Gospel and our way of living. What is discovered in this study shows a startling contrast between the principles on which most of one's conduct has been based and the principles laid down in the Gospel by Our Divine Lord. There follows on this discovery, feelings of uneasiness, shame, terror and a keen desire to escape from the un-Christian state of soul in which one finds oneself. The newly awakened soul is startled to find that in reality it had been living its life as if the Gospel and its principles were meant to apply only in a partial measure to itself, and were reserved in their literal application only to some rare beings with a special vocation to be saints.

It is truly disconcerting to find that there is but one Gospel for all and that one has to conform oneself to that, or face the most severe consequences here and hereafter. Without deliberately formulating it as a theory, the average person practically works out a comfortable kind of Gospel for himself, bearing but a faint resemblance to that of Jesus Christ. In other words people who are not definitely converted to God, Christians who allow themselves to be carried away by the worldly and false life around them, come to justify views, principles and a course of action which find no justification in the teaching of Jesus Christ. " God is hidden in us, and from us," writes St. John of the Cross. " To find Him we must go to hide ourselves where He is hidden. In other words to find God, we must forget ourselves completely, separate ourselves from all creatures and retire within our own interior. Then having renounced all, we can pray to the Father in secret."[1] The beginnings of the Presence of God are very painful and demand

[1] St. John of the Cross. 1st Strophe of " The Dark Night of the Soul ".

strong efforts, for sin (and the habits it engenders) has sown such discord in the original relations between the soul and its Creator, that we are in truth strangers to God—strangers to Him who is our First Principle and our Last End—as if an abyss separated us from Him in whom we live, move and have our being.

"We have been so accustomed," says St. Teresa, "to follow every whim and fancy, to gratify ourselves in all that we consider not positively sinful (our efforts to live a Christian life have consisted rather in the effort to avoid what was wrong, than to do what was right)² that the soul no longer understands itself as a soul. To accustom it to God it is necessary to proceed slowly, with caution and patience."³

A vivid realisation of the falsity of its attitude towards life is the first strong grace given to the soul when it resolves to turn to God. The work that is demanded from it, if it is to profit by that grace, is that it should form strong, deep and practical convictions on this one point—namely that the type of life portrayed by Our Lord is the only one that can be adopted by oneself if one is to be Christian.⁴ Owing to ingrained habits, the soul finds an active rebellion in itself against the acceptation of this life as its own. Mental Prayer at this point is made up chiefly of considerations; the activity is mostly of the understanding; the rôle of the will is limited. The acts of the latter are mostly of repentance, an earnest pleading for forgiveness

---

² The words in parenthesis are mine.

³ *Way of Perfection*—St. Teresa. Chap. xxvi.

⁴ In speaking of adopting the type of life led by Our Lord, the words are not to be taken in a material sense. To adopt the Lord's life does not involve taking up the occupation of His earthly existence, but it means living our life after the principles which guided His.

for the past which looms now in horror against the vivid light which God has projected on the background of the previous existence. The soul with a deep sense of its own sinfulness pours itself out in humble petitions for help to improve. The Lord listens patiently, contemplates with pity, says very little on His side (for the soul cannot as yet understand the Divine instructions) but accords an increased taste for spiritual things, a detestation of worldly things, and the grace of strong repentance. The soul begins little by little to see itself as God sees it, because it has learned to make its considerations as if analysing itself in the presence of the Divine Master. Even when engaged in an examination of its own states and dispositions it must not turn its gaze away from the Lord or lose the sense of His presence. It must examine itself, as it were, through His eyes and in His light.

The soul leaves the presence of Jesus with the resolution to practise the virtues which it has seen in Him and to uproot the vices it has now discovered in itself. It succeeds as long as the movement of fervour lasts and is cheated by this success into the belief that it is already on the high road to sanctity. The soul having an imperfect notion of the action of prayer, falls into the mistake of thinking that it can have virtues for the mere asking of them and rid itself of its defects by praying for such an emancipation. It does not realise that to acquire the former and rid itself of the latter, there is required a long process and much labour and toil. To extirpate a vice requires a constant unremitting reaction against its activity, by continual exercise of the acts of the opposite virtue.

The soul does not readily understand this, and very
easily, in a sense of false security due to the excesses
of fervour it has experienced, it allows itself to drift
into ways and modes of action incompatible with
the interior life. It yields to dissipation, distraction
and immortification without adverting to the fact
that these faults rapidly undermine the frail spiritual
edifice it has constructed. The old habits have not,
as it thinks, been burned away and destroyed in the
fervour of sensible devotion. Their activities have
been dormant for a time but they have remained
strongly rooted in the soul. The consequence is that
when the fervour has passed and the normal play of
circumstances begins, and occasions arise, things forthwith make the same appeal to the appetites as before.

Very few realise that every mortal sin leaves on
the soul a strong tendency to evil—sets up in it a
perverse disposition which does not disappear with
the tears of repentance and the sentence of pardon.
The habits created by years of the self-indulgence
of a worldly life do not disappear in the fervour of
a well-made retreat. Unless one is on the watch and
exercises oneself in mortification, these habits begin
to manifest themselves when the circumstances are
favourable to their excitation. The things that pleased
of old begin to exercise the same attraction again ;
and in corresponding measure the taste for spiritual
things declines. The inexperienced soul is astonished
and dismayed at finding as active in itself as ever the
evil tendencies which it believed had disappeared
for ever. In the renewed contact with the evil in itself,
all the period of fervour begins to appear to have

been a time of unreality. Having begun the supernatural enterprise under a false notion, it becomes
discouraged and loses confidence in itself. It has erred
in confusing sensible devotion with spirituality.

God gives sensible fervour in order to enable us
to break more readily with our vicious habits. Being
immortified we are drawn towards that which is most
attractive for us. God, stooping to this weakness
and profiting by it in the interests of our salvation,
gives us a sensible attraction to spiritual things and
shows us natural things in a light which renders them
distasteful. By this illumination we are enabled to
form a conviction of the superiority of the good of
the soul over any merely natural good. This conviction is made to enable us to persevere afterwards
when all becomes dark.

Spirituality itself has no attraction for nature; on the
contrary nature is repelled by it. Our progress in the
spiritual life is in direct proportion to the degree in
which nature[5] has been brought into subjection. Now,
if the sensible attraction for spiritual things were to
continue to exist, our nature, that is, the appetite for
self-gratification in us, would be nourished by it and
would not die. God, to wean the soul from seeking
its gratification in creatures, offers it in the beginning
a gratification of a superior kind derived from spiritual
things. But the soul cannot make progress unless
it aims at spirituality independently of any gratification

---

[5] The word ' nature ' here is to be taken in the ascetical, not in the exact
philosophical sense. It means what St. Catherine of Siena calls sensuality.
It is the ' ensemble ' of these tendencies both of the spirit and the senses,
in which man aims at procuring his own satisfaction, independently of the
law both of reason and of faith.

it finds in it. Hence to cure it of its " spiritual sensual-ity ", God withdraws sensible delight in the interior life and leaves the soul to go forward in faith. The soul then finds itself faced with the evil habits and tendencies fostered by a life lived for the gratification of self. To conquer these habits and develop the supernatural virtues of religion, humility, charity and mortification, God leaves the beginner in the spiritual life with merely the firm conviction, based upon faith, of the necessity of acquiring the virtues just mentioned, of advancing in the grace of God and saving his soul.

In this state it is evident that things will act upon the individual in the way in which they were wont to act. The soul is affected by things precisely in the same way as it was affected by them previous to its conversion. It is readily drawn towards what is opposed to the life of the spirit, and it has no attraction towards the acts and habits that pertain to the life of virtue. It has nothing to move it to the practice of christian virtue except the rational conviction, enlightened by faith, of the utility and the necessity of virtue if it is to attain to union with God.

This is a moment of serious danger in the spiritual life. It is a point where great numbers turn aside and quit the path that leads to intimacy with God. Mortifica-tion, the avoidance of occasions that tempt to dissipation or sensuality and the strong resolve to cling to God even though His service involve only hardship and distastefulness—these are the safeguards against failure. But if one is weak, if one allows oneself to drift into the ways frequented before, if one seeks the same satisfactions in pleasant companionships and indulges in the practices of the previous immortified life, if one permits sensuality, waste of time, self-indulgence and self-seeking to invade one's life, the inevitable happens. The supernatural becomes a vague unreal memory, a dream from which one has awakened to reality. The conviction of its importance is obliterated and all the good effects produced during the period of fervour disappear. Having been accustomed to doing always that which is agreeable and to avoid what is disagreeable, the soul gives up spirituality as soon as it ceases to exercise an attraction on it. The soul longed to find in spirituality a bread pleasing to the sensible palate and so falls victim to the temptations of sensuality. The soul at this juncture undergoes a struggle that bears a resemblance to the first temptation of Our Saviour in the desert. The temptation is to renounce the pursuit of union with God when there is no longer any " felt " or experienced satisfaction in that pursuit. It is the temptation to ask that the stones that go to make up the rugged path that leads to God, the hard stones of mortification and self-denial, change their nature and be turned into something agreeable to the palate of the natural man.

This temptation is very strong and many souls fall victims to it. It is all the more subtle because it seems so reasonable. To the soul, finding in itself a positive distaste for what appears to be the cold forbidding deserts of the spiritual life and finding in itself on the other hand a very strong inclination for and a drawing towards the pleasures of the natural life, it seems absurd to continue the pursuit of an ideal for which its experiences apparently manifest its unfitness. The former efforts after a practice of Christianity above the ordinary now appear the effect of a vain and mistaken ambition. The soul does not "feel" itself to be spiritual, why should it continue to act in the way spiritual persons act? Why not satisfy the natural longings (of course always within the limits of the Ten Commandments) —why not "command the stones to be made bread" and live like everybody else? Carried away by these reasonings the soul gives up the practice of the interior life altogether or becomes slack and perfunctory in the exercise of that life. Its ambition gradually dwindles down to what it thinks to be the observance of the decalogue; the observance of the ordinary law of God as interpreted by itself is sufficient spirituality, it thinks, for one of its humble attainments and unspiritual tastes; it is effort enough to keep within the limits of the main points of Christian law. It persuades itself that salvation may be secured by these limited efforts without facing the hardships of an austere interior life. For a soul that has received the call to close intimacy with God such a resolve may prove fatal.

As the temptation bears a resemblance to that of Jesus in the desert, the resistance to it must be such as His was. "Not on bread alone doth man live but on every word that proceedeth from the mouth of God."[6] Bread is undoubtedly the staff of life. But the life that it maintains is not the only·one that is

[6] St. Matt. iv. 4.

given to man to live. Life can have a higher form, and nourishment of another kind. If we seek for a "life that is truly life"—and that is what we are really seeking—we must give up looking for it in the eating of bread, that is, in the pursuit of those things that are agreeable to the appetite of the natural man. This seeking after and the giving oneself every possible gratification, short of those that involve a grave breach of God's law, does give a certain kind of life, but this life is as nothing compared with that which is enjoyed by feeding our souls on the word of God. Life is to be sought only where it is to be found lastingly; it is so found in intimacy with God, in converse with Him, in nourishing our souls on His communications. Life is to be found for us in the words that proceed from the mouth of God and are addressed to the spirit within. Convinced of the fundamental truth that we are created to praise, revere and serve God, convinced that we belong to Him absolutely whether we will it or no, we must be resolved to persevere in fulfilling His will in our regard,— which will is our sanctification[7]—even though everything that the fulfilment of that will involves, prove distasteful to us. We must be ready to pursue the work of our own sanctification, even though we are sorely tried by hunger after the satisfactions of a life lived for the indulgence of every gratification not positively sinful. We must be strong to rise superior to our feelings and to follow not that which is more pleasant, but that which conducts us most surely and securely to God's friendship.

[7] "This is the will of God, your sanctification" (1 Thess. iv. 3).

The discipline of the religious life, resolutely submitted to, is a great help in this crisis. The rule calls to the exercise of prayer several times in the day; it enjoins an attention and a reverential posture at these exercises; in this way it saves the soul from a complete surrender to itself. If the sorely tempted soul were free to regulate the activities of its day, it would, probably, abandon the practise of mental prayer altogether as being tedious and unfruitful.

There is a definite course of conduct to be followed in this trial if the danger it carries with it is to be escaped. The person that has begun to walk in the way of the interior life, must continue to acquit himself of his exercises of prayer with fidelity and with all the perfection, at least material and exterior, that he brought to their acquittal when carried away by a strong movement of devotion and fervour. He must do them even though he finds no apparent good in his prayer, even though he has no satisfaction in it, even though he has a positive distaste for it. In a word though he finds himself in no way ' prayerful ', he must ' act as if ' he were. Those who are at this point in the interior life must not allow themselves to be betrayed into making their outward bearing reflect what they think to be their inner attitude of soul. Though they feel as if all their spirituality had oozed away from their soul, they must continue to bear themselves in their relations with persons or things, and especially their spiritual exercises, as they did when fervent. The salutary effect of this will be felt speedily, for there is a natural reaction of the exterior on the interior. There is a great virtue in this principle of " acting as if ". Men tend to develop feelings corresponding to their actions. The successful effort to wear a smiling countenance induces an inner disposition of pleasantness and amiability. Thoughts in their turn are influenced by feelings and finally actions bear the impress of thoughts. It is by the working of this psychological law that a spiritual bearing and deportment, as, for instance, a deliberately reverential attitude in the presence of God, a christian dignity and elevation in speech, and a courteous attitude towards others, are instrumental in producing a true, inward devotion. For all this, of course, there are needed, courage, energy and self-discipline.

The earnest and upright soul must not allow itself to be betrayed into the belief that in acting in the manner outlined it will be behaving in an unreal and hypocritical manner. It is a common temptation to judge that it is dishonest not to bear oneself outwardly as one is (or believes one is) inwardly. This judgment contains a profound error. There are in us two selves, the true and the false. We are more conscious of the latter than the former, and that is the reason why the false appears to us to be the real self. By Baptism we have been made children of God and have ceased to be children of wrath. The true self in us, in consequence, is the child of grace, the brother of Jesus Christ. The alien from God has been thrust out by Baptism, ostracized, and condemned to death. " You are not," says St. Paul, writing to the Romans, " in the flesh, but in the spirit . . . and if Christ be in you, the body indeed is dead because of sin, but the spirit liveth because of justification . . . therefore, brethren, we are debtors not to the flesh, to live according to the flesh."[8] We are really false in our bearing and untrue to ourselves when we act and speak according to the unspiritual promptings in us. That character is not acting hypocritically but acting in the very reverse manner, who carries himself outwardly in all the relations of life, as a being that is spiritual, of heavenly tastes, though he "feels" anything but that interiorly. Furthermore, by constantly acting "spiritually" he becomes "spiritual".[9]

When Satan, urging this argument of hypocrisy, bids us be such as we find ourselves, he must be met by a counter argument. He said to the Lord, "Why depend on God for your food, why not use the power that is really yours and make these stones be bread?" The Saviour answered that though there was in Him a life that was sustained by bread, there was another and a higher life that was sustained by loving dependence on and union with God. So likewise, when Satan whispers to us that we are really but sinful creatures, with earthly tastes and likings, and that we should,

---

[8] Rom. viii. 9–12.

[9] It may be noted that it is equally true according to this psychological law that by exteriorly acting in an " unspiritual way " one becomes unspiritual. This fact frequently becomes of practical importance in the spiritual life. The tendency to " take the line of least resistance ", to be accommodating, to respond to the dictates of human respect, often leads souls to assume a course of action or agree with a course of thought which is distinctly unspiritual and even worldly. Such " putting on " is meant to be " for the time being ", but apart from the fact that it means a definite relinquishing of principles, it has the sad result of developing the facility to be worldly and unspiritual and of producing a mentality that is by no means Christlike. The truth of this is exemplified in the case of religious who in contact with the world (the parlour or hospital) assume the ways and line of thought of those who are not in religion and whose lives are not completely influenced by the principles of Christ Our Lord. If spiritual progress is to be made the soul must adopt the advice of St. John Berchmans :—" Make open profession of aiming at the interior life ".

if sincere and honest, act as such, our reply should have a parallelism with that of the Saviour's. " True," we should say to him, " we are sinful creatures, but we are not only that. We have been redeemed. By right and title we are children of God." That is what we really and truly are; the other we have been. To act then as it becomes us to act, truly to reflect in our conduct what we are, we must in all things comport ourselves as having heavenly tastes and ideals. It is to be admitted that years of seeking after gratification have developed in us tastes the very opposite of those that befit a child of God. At present, owing to the habits formed by the years of self-indulgence, I find interiorly a contradiction between my true and my false self, and the latter seems to be predominant. Yet by the cultivation of a truly spiritual bearing in all things possible to me by ascetical effort aided by grace, I know that this contradiction will ultimately disappear. The exterior will finally affect the interior; the old habits will wither away and I shall end by finding satisfaction in God alone. My life will be the living by every word that proceeds from the mouth of God. When the soul has in this manner rejected the wiles of Satan, she has taken a decisive step onward in the interior life.

It is because many souls are persuaded that they should reflect in their exterior what they conceive to be their true, but what is in reality their false self, that there is the too common spectacle of those who having begun well end by being complete failures spiritually. The arguments of Satan, condemning as hypocrisy, this effort to " act as if spiritual," must be treated as a temptation and met by counter arguments. The truth is that the Christian is by Baptism a child of God and should therefore have an interior disposition corresponding to that state. He should have affection only for God and for all else in God. When conversion is at its beginning, the evil habits that have been contracted by a past life lived for self, give us tastes quite opposite to the tastes that should be those of a child of God. Those heavenly tastes and instincts cannot become rooted in the soul until the contrary ones have been rooted out. That rooting out will involve time and labour. But in the meantime whilst awaiting the successful termination of the process of destroying the perverse tendencies, the Christian can school himself to act as if the process were complete. He must so bear himself as if his tastes were all spiritual, avoiding such speech, such acts, such judgment, such courses of conduct as mark the non-spiritual.

CHAPTER VII

" It is written—thou shalt adore the Lord thy God and Him only shalt thou serve." St. Luke iv. 8.

THE soul having thus successfully surmounted the first great trial in the interior life returns to God with the conviction that it must serve Him, not for the delight it finds in the things appertaining to His service but solely for His sake and for the sake of union with Him as the end for which it has been created. It is now clearly seen that seeking God is not a matter of delight but of a steady struggle to overcome defects, root out vices and practise virtues. With this end in view, prayer takes on a new tone. Already in the first stage strong and deep convictions have been formed with regard to fundamental truths. The soul now occupies itself seriously with the means of realising the consequences that flow from these basic truths. The principal of these consequences is that God must be won at all costs and that the life which does not issue in close union with Him is a failure. Acts of sorrow and regret are still frequent, but they have changed somewhat their tone and character. Formerly they proceeded principally from a hatred of the acts of sin because of the evil consequences they involved, now repentance tends to become a dislike of sin as being destructive of the moral beauty the soul aspires to.

The soul realises its own fundamental weakness; it sees that the source of its sins lies deeper than it

thought at first. It thought it had only to make an
act of the will in order to be good. It thought that
it had only to will to change and immediately spiritual
tastes would replace the earthly ones. It finds that
it can will and will very strongly to change and yet
no change follows. It believed that there was nothing
more in sin than the act, and that with the cessation
of the act would disappear the root of the sins. It
has not yet realised that the habit of self-will and self-
indulgence is rooted out only by a long course of self-
denial. The evil that it still finds strong in itself makes
it understand that its own conversion to good has
not destroyed in it the source of corruption. It has
become clear that this source can be dried up only
by a laborious pursuit and practice of the acts of the
virtues contrary to the vices it finds rooted in itself.
It knows too that its own efforts count little but that
much can be achieved by the help of the Divine Master.
It trusts to His goodness for that help. Its chief aim
at this stage, becomes the acquisition of the virtues
and it sets itself to a study of the means to acquire
these virtues and to overcome the opposite vices.

The soul becomes ardently eager for its own
perfection and feels a deep humiliation and shame at
its imperfections. It asks the Lord earnestly to assist
it to acquire these virtues and to raise it to the perfection
it ambitions. Souls at this point often experience
an acute spiritual jealousy of others whom they see
advanced in the way of perfection; they are pained
at the humiliating contrast presented by their own
miserable state. This ambition and jealousy show
that there is a large measure of self-love and self-esteem

in the desire to become perfect. They importune
Our Lord, more because they desire to see themselves perfect, than to see God served. Acts of virtue
are frequent. The soul gives itself eagerly to the
practice of them, because it has confidence that it can,
with God's co-operation, attain the end it has set before
itself. The life of Jesus forms the ordinary subject
of meditation. The soul desires to contemplate Him
in the practice of the different virtues, in order to
stimulate itself to the desire of them and to learn how
to practise them after the manner of its Divine Model.
The Lord, on His side, co-operates more strongly
—impressing the imagination powerfully with the details
of His mysteries and forming the intelligence to a more
perfect understanding of the principles underlying His
life on earth. The soul is carried away by the beauty
and desirability of a life lived after the pattern He has
traced. When in prayer, owing to the strong way it is
affected by the beauty of the conduct it contemplates,
it believes itself strong against its own weakness and
it thinks that it can easily imitate the Lord's virtue.
Outside of prayer it finds its weakness. It believes
itself at times to be virtuous but fails under test. Pained
at its own failure and seeing in prayer alone a remedy,
it returns to it with eagerness and multiplies its petitions.
The acts of the will become more numerous and
gradually replace in prominence the acts of the intellect.
The Lord gives good inspirations in plenty. His
direction is stronger and more manifest. The virtues
begin to grow feebly because the soul is schooling
itself to act under the inspiration of grace and is
partially successful. The rule of life is carefully observed ;

the soul is attentive to inspirations, but is still full of the seeds of faults. These escape it on many occasions—especially faults of impatience, irritation and jealousy. The habit of prayer however, grows and the practice of it becomes less difficult.

By the aid of the particular examination it succeeds occasionally for a certain length of time in producing the acts of one or other of the virtues. This temporary success lulls it into security and cheats it into the belief that the virtue in question is firmly rooted in the soul. A sudden surprise, an encounter not prepared for, causes it to relapse into impatience, uncharitableness, irritability, jealousy, etc., and it realises with keen disappointment that the virtue it fondly hoped that it possessed is yet far from being acquired.

The days as they pass, witness a constant alternation of these successes and failures. The spiritual combat is a series of beginnings. After much effort little progress is to be noted, apparently. The soul finds itself as prone to criticism, ill temper, sensuality, etc. as ever. It begins to wonder why the Lord shows Himself so deaf to its appeals and allows it to remain a prey to its vices and defects. It cannot reconcile the continued refusal, as it seems to it to be, to accord it the virtues it pleads for so humbly, earnestly and perseveringly, with the Lord's promise to give whatever should be asked for in prayer. Tested by actual experience how can His words "Ask and you shall receive"[1] be found to be true? The soul has asked again and again, and it has not received.

[1] St. John xvi. 24.

This is the ordinary state of good souls. Their faults are numerous enough but their conscience is delicate and reproaches them for any want of generosity in God's service. The source of their failures is to be traced to their want of detachment from creatures but especially detachment from themselves. Their notion of holiness evinces that, for they pursue not so much the service of God as their own perfection. They do not want to be miserable and imperfect, their self-love rebels against that. Hence, they pursue virtue for its own sake, and they hate vice because it is degrading and ugly. Nevertheless the action of the Lord is strong upon them and increases continually whilst the action of the soul, hitherto somewhat feverish and full of natural effort, becomes calmer and less complex. The prayer tends to become more affective and has fewer and simpler considerations. In the light of the illuminations the soul receives from its Divine guide and director, it observes in itself defects which would before have passed unobserved or which would have been regarded as not worth considering. The Lord reproaches it for any infidelities and especially for any natural attachments that it tends to allow itself to contract. It is given clearly to understand that the Lord will not have a divided heart and that His love demands perfect detachment.

The danger for the soul at this juncture is serious, for it can become ensnared by its own striving after perfection. It is sincere in its belief that it is actuated by an earnest desire to draw closer to God. But in reality since it has as yet made little progress in detachment, its love of God is not pure. It contains a heavy mixture of alloy. It is its own goodness, its own perfection, its own purity that the soul is enamoured of. The ideal of " itself perfect " draws it and inspires its efforts. God of course is not excluded from this ideal for the call to perfection comes from God, and it is in obedience to this call that the spiritual enterprise has been engaged in. But not having as yet a clear idea of what constitutes its perfection, the soul unwittingly is drawn on, mainly by the anxiety to see itself equipped with virtue. Its own moral beauty, seen in thought as an object capable of being realised by the aid of God, is what the soul is in love with.[2] It thinks that this moral excellence is what God has appointed to it as an end to strive after. The snare is a subtle one. It is not easy for the inexperienced to see that there is a refined self-love involved in this struggle after virtue, or rather after " oneself virtuous ". It is God, not virtue, that must be loved since virtue is a means not an end. Not seeing this clearly, the soul is, unawares, really captivated by an ideal that is human and created. The weakness generated in the soul by this, leaves it exposed to be captivated by other forms of created good and to seek its satisfaction therein. The devil seizes his opportunity to ensnare it by one of its predominant tendencies. The soul is easily led to form an obstinate attachment to its own excellence proposed to it under the guise that makes the strongest appeal to its temperament. The

---

[2] The form of vanity described here and which is such a common obstacle (especially for women) is ruthlessly denounced by St. John of the Cross. Max. 324. " There are many Christians in our day who have certain virtues and who do great things, but all of no use to them in the matter of everlasting life because in them they do not seek that honour and glory which belongs to God alone, but rather the empty satisfaction of their own will."

ambitious soul is carried away by the desire of praise, of success, of position. The pursuit of all this will be made to appear as in line with one's progress in perfection and the service of God. The affectionate and attractive soul will be tempted to exercise its power and to attach others to itself—ostensibly in the interests of God. The cold and upright will be easily betrayed into a spirit of self-righteousness, domineering, harshness of judgment, uncharitableness and want of consideration for others. Because of the love of self that has insinuated itself into its pursuit of virtue the soul may readily fall a victim to one or other of these temptations.

There is still another and a common danger to which it is exposed through this base alloy of self-love that is mixed with its love of God. Just as it is attracted by that created object—its own excellence, so it may easily be drawn to the real or fancied good in other creatures. At this stage the soul owing to its imperfection can easily form attachments to creatures. These attachments are usually based upon the discernment of real excellence in the object. The soul accustomed to love its own excellence easily succumbs to the attraction of excellence in others. The affection called forth by what is really good, will appear to be justifiable and according to God. It often has, in fact, spiritual beginnings. But such attachments to creatures, no matter how good, will, at this stage of the soul's progress, eventually degenerate into something really harmful. The good that is loved remains a created good. An idol is set up on the heart alongside of God. The inordinate love of the created cannot exist by the side of the love of the Creator.[3] The Holy Ghost is driven from His rightful place and the soul becomes insensible to His inspirations. Spiritual progress is impeded and retrogression begins. What is more dangerous still is that this retrogression is imperceptible and will have reached an advanced stage before it arouses attention. The reason is that the soul, having acquired, by its previous efforts, habits of regularity of prayer and of other pious practices, does not lose these habits immediately. It can continue for a considerable time invested with the outward form of spirituality, after the inner spirit has taken its departure.[4]

This temptation to love a created excellence in oneself or others—an excellence that is wrongly thought to be closely connected with the attractiveness of God —marks a decisive moment in the interior life. Our Divine Lord has shown us how to resist it. We must be always on our guard and never rely to any extent on the progress we have made. Attachments to self in any of the ways above mentioned have slight and often imperceptible beginnings and before it is aware the soul is entangled. To avoid this disaster the soul must never allow itself to rest in any created thing no matter how good. Even its own holiness and excellence is not to be pursued as an end. Even that must remain simply a means to God. "And Jesus answering said to him: It is written; thou shalt adore the Lord thy God, and Him only shalt thou serve."[5] Satan

---

[3] "The sources of the waters of interior joy are not on earth; the mouth of desire must be opened heavenwards, utterly empty." St. John of the Cross, Letter ii.

[4] Cf. St. Fr. de Sales. *Love of God*, iv. 9.

[5] St. Luke iv. 8.

unveiled to the Saviour's gaze the whole realm of created loveliness. There was much in that vision to attract and subjugate the human heart. The appeal of beauty is very strong and it is not the ignoble but the gifted and idealistic that are most sensitive to that appeal. There are few that would appreciate as the Saviour did the attractiveness that stood revealed to Him in the whole realm of nature that was spread before His gaze. The tempter thought that the Man who stood before him would be conquered by that attractiveness, made a slave to it and weaned thereby from the charm of the Creator of it all. He thought that by an inordinate affection Jesus would be made the slave of the creature and withdrawn from subjection to God. He was utterly mistaken. Jesus loved what He saw, but loved it in God and not as a substitute for or in the place of God. Before God only would He prostrate Himself. To Him only would He offer the worship of His love. To His beauty only would He acknowledge Himself a slave.

The soul that is determined to go forward in the interior life must be on its guard against all attachments to creatures. There are, of course, human affections which are in the plan of God and blessed by Him. There is no question of these legitimate affections, but of the ones that are called inordinate. These latter either not being according to God or not observing the measure ordained by God, necessarily oust God from the soul and take His place. Even good souls are susceptible to beauty in the various forms in which it presents itself. They are susceptible to beauty of mind, to beauty of soul and to beauty

of the external form. The beauty in inanimate nature
and the splendours of art in its various forms can
exercise a strong sway over them. Pious souls are
prone to be strongly drawn towards those whom they
think have been for them an inspiration to good and
whose qualities of mind or soul they admire. In all
these cases, there is the appeal of created beauty to
the soul most sensitive to that appeal. There is danger
of enslavement. As long as there is a strong attachment
to self in the soul—and at this stage there is such an
attachment—it is almost morally impossible that its
love for others will not be tainted with selfishness.
It is almost certain therefore that it will be inordinate
and impair the friendship with God. We can love
creatures properly only when our love is disinterested.
We love them as we should, when we love them in
God and for His sake. As long as we are lovers of
self in our tendency towards God, there is danger
that the affection we contract for creatures will be
inordinate. We shall love creatures purely when we
love God purely. That will be when we love God
with perfect detachment from self. It is then and then
only that we can safely pour out our affections on
creatures. We attach ourselves to creatures without
danger when we are perfectly detached from them
and from ourselves. The inordinate affections of
which there has been question can have relation to
every created attraction that can warm the human
imagination. Those who have made headway in
spirituality by the overcoming of their sensuality
can become enslaved to riches, honours, distinctions,
positions, the esteem of others, as well as to the beauty,

mental or physical, of those who have charm of mind
or body. If the soul is to advance, it must be jealous
of its freedom. It must maintain complete liberty
with regard to all creature charms at any cost. It must
be resolute in the determination not to allow itself to be
subjugated by any charm except the charm of God.[6]

[6] (a) "The immense treasures of God can only be contained in a heart
which is empty and solitary". St. John of the Cross. Max. 349. (b) The
solitariness or detachment which is needed is well summarised by St. Francis
de Sales :—"Indifference ought to be practised in everything which relates
to natural life, such as health, sickness, beauty, ugliness, weakness or strength ;
in all things concerning civil life, honours, ranks and riches ; in all the
varieties of the spiritual life ; as dryness, consolation, sweetness in prayer,
aridity ; in all our actions, sufferings and every kind of happening ". *Love
of God,* ix. 5.

CHAPTER VIII

THE THIRD STAGE IN THE TRANSFORMATION

" It is said—thou shalt not tempt the Lord thy God."
St. Luke iv. 12.

WHEN the soul has conquered its sensuality, when moreover it has succeeded in maintaining the heart free for God, when it has kept itself faithful to its resolve to find God at all costs, and has arrived at the renouncement of all affections that are not in God and for God—and thus has attained the detachment towards which the Lord has been directing it—it reaches the third stage in the interior life, a stage that has characteristics which distinguish it sharply from the other two.

The soul has learned by experience, that all its efforts after the acquisition of the virtues have had very little success; time and time again, when the occasions offered themselves of practising those virtues which at moments it thought it had acquired, it failed abjectly; it failed in patience, submission, humility, simplicity and charity. The conviction has at last been forced upon it—a conviction which the Lord has been all the time trying to bring home to it—that it is, of itself, by its own efforts, incapable of any good at all, much less of acquiring virtue.

The discovery has not, however, the effect of causing it any discouragement or irritation—both signs of pride. For its detachment has earned for it the great grace of a perfect confidence, that if it submits itself absolutely to His action the Lord can accomplish in

it these things to which it aspires, that He can effect
in it the virtues it has been struggling to acquire.

At last the truth has dawned on it that perfection
is not its own work, or to be acquired by its own
efforts, but is purely the work of Our Divine Lord
Whom St. Teresa loves to compare to a gardener
working in the soul. The moment that the soul realises
that it is absolutely incapable of attaining to goodness,
is precisely the moment of salvation for it, if this
complete distrust in itself is accompanied by an
unbounded trust in the Lord's power to effect sanctification in the creatures He has redeemed by His
blood.[1]

The soul sees that its own co-operation in the work
consists solely in divesting itself of self by the practice
of self-abnegation, and by foregoing whatever would
attach it or enslave it to any creature. It understands
that its rôle in the work of sanctification consists in
holding itself free from all ties in order that the Lord
may operate freely in it. It sees that what is required
of it is to combat all inordinate affections and to attach
itself exclusively to God. It still falls into frequent
faults, because it is still very imperfect, but these
passing failures neither astonish nor wound, nor
irritate nor cause disappointment. They are clearly

[1] Compare the following passage from Newman. "Those whom Christ
saves are they who at once attempt to save themselves, yet despair of saving
themselves; who aim to do all and confess that they do naught; who are
all love and all fear; who are the most holy, yet confess themselves the
most sinful; who ever seek to please Him, yet feel they never can; who
are full of good works, yet works of penance. All this seems a contradiction
to the natural man, but it is not so to those whom Christ enlightens. They
understand, in proportion to their illumination, that it is possible to work
out their salvation, yet to have it wrought out for them, to fear and tremble
at the thought of judgment, yet to rejoice always in the hour and hope and
pray for His coming." Newman *P.S.* vii. 12.

seen to rise from those depths of the soul as yet unsubmitted to God. The soul realises keenly that this fundamental weakness will show itself as soon as it releases its hold on the hand of Jesus. But these lapses do not cause despair of ultimate success; the soul seizes each lapse as an occasion for plunging itself deeper and deeper into humility, and of clinging with more and more tenacity to the help and companionship of Jesus. It asks pardon, resolves to be with Him more frequently, to keep closer to Him and begin again with unabated courage and perfect peace. If the soul does any good it assigns it readily to the Lord, for it has been clearly shown that it is He alone that operates any good; if it does wrong, commits faults, it recognises that nothing else is to be expected from unregenerate human nature. The soul is illuminated to its depths by the truth contained in the Lord's words —" I am the vine; you the branches; he that abideth in me and I in him, the same beareth much fruit; for without me you can do nothing."[2] It has become very patient with itself, and fully expects that the Lord will in the end replace its own vileness with His goodness. The process may take years but it is confident that that end will come, if in the meantime detachment and docility of life are practised.[3]

At this stage prayer has come to be of extreme simplicity; a mere glance at the subject of meditation suffices to put the intelligence in possession of

[2] St. John xv. 5.
[3] By docility of life is meant an uncomplaining submission to all the dispensations of Divine Providence, accepting everything that comes to one as coming from God's Hand and as being meant to work towards one's sanctification.

the points, and of their bearing on the particular
state in which the soul happens to find itself. Considerations are no longer necessary; convictions have
been formed, and the soul is desirous of nothing except
of pleasing God and of advancing in friendship with
Him, pursuing virtue merely as a means to this. The
whole exercise tends to develop into a simple, familiar
and intimate conversation with Jesus. The soul has
now taken its own worthlessness for granted, and
is no longer so much enamoured with the idea or
prospect of its own excellence. Its objective is entirely
changed; it aims no longer at its own perfection as
an end but at the love and service of God. It asks
for perfection, but its request is purely disinterested;
it is asked for simply because the soul sees in it an
indispensable means towards serving God properly.
The soul has at last ceased to be self-centred in its
pursuit of perfection, and has become God-centred.
It surrenders itself entirely to the action of the Lord,
begging Him to transform it to His own likeness
and to impress His own virtues upon it. Sufferings
are no longer merely patiently borne—they commence
to be valued; they are recognised to be most efficacious instruments in the working out of perfect detachment from creatures, and in purifying the soul from
all attachment to self. The action or direction of the
Lord now becomes very pronounced, and the gifts
of the Holy Ghost exercise increased activity.

The soul has become very mobile to the action
of the Holy Spirit. The self-analysis characteristic
of the former states disappears. Only one ambition
now stirs the soul, namely that of lending itself as

an instrument, to be used by the Lord to effect His purposes. It bewails its imperfections for the reason that they destroy or mar its perfection as an instrument, making it less serviceable. It, therefore, presents itself readily to the purifying action of the Divine Will which tempers and perfects it in the fire of trial and suffering. The Lord becomes the chief worker; and the action of the soul consists in the loving desire to serve God at all costs, and a docile surrender to Him to equip it for that service. The soul has become much more childlike in its attitude towards the Lord, in its attitude of complete dependence on Him and perfect confidence in Him.[4]

Its objective has undergone a complete change unconsciously. Zeal for the glory of God and the accomplishment of His will, in itself, in others and over the whole earth, has replaced its passionate ardour for its own good and its own perfection. The action of the theological virtue of charity dominates that of the virtue of hope. It has become to a great extent oblivious of self and its own concerns, and begins to be more occupied with the interests of God Whom it loves. It is not that it is obliged to make

[4] The dispositions that characterise the soul at this stage are well set forth in the following passage, translated from *La Vie Spirituelle*—Jan. 1923. " It will not be out of place to review the qualities of this spiritual childhood, either in what it excludes or in what it presupposes. It excludes in fact the dominating idea of self, the presumption that we attain by human means to a supernatural end, the deceptive fancy of self-sufficiency at the time of peril and temptation. On the other hand, it presupposes a lively faith in the existence of God, a practical adoration of His power and mercy, a confident recourse to the Providence of Him who grants us the grace to avoid evil and do good. Thus the qualities of this spiritual childhood are excellent, whether regarded from the negative or positive point of view, and hence one understands how Our Lord has marked it out as a necessary condition to obtain eternal life."

efforts to leave self out of count or to forget self;
but preoccupied as it is, about God, it ceases without
observing it, to think about self at all. The absence
of self-consciousness, the characteristic of that childlike simplicity that Our Lord demands as a condition
of entrance into intimacy with Him, develops with
the growth of charity; this want of self-consciousness
precludes to a great extent the necessity of that active
and positive repression of self which constituted the
chief work of the soul in the two previous stages.
The acquisition of simplicity does away with the
necessity of self-repression—for self is no longer
assertive.

According as this self-consciousness disappears there
is developed a consciousness of another kind—namely,
a growing realisation of the great truth that one is
not a mere isolated individual, but forms part of a
great mystical organism in the life of which the individual shares. The Catholic sense is gradually replacing
the individual sense. The soul now aims at conforming
its thoughts and its feelings with those of that
Mystical *Body* with whom it feels itself identified in
the community of a common life. Its previous
experience and study has revealed to it fully the inner
dispositions, aspirations and devotion of the Head
of that Body, of that Head which imparts to the Body
all the vitality it has in the supernatural order.[5] The

---

[5] An intelligent grasp and appreciation of the principles which motived
the life of Christ; an earnest application of these principles in the living
of our human lives, results (with God's grace) in that ideal conformity
to which we are bound to aspire. But of these even who study the life of
our Lord—and study it prayerfully—comparatively few approach it to
find a unified grasp of the principles according to which Jesus lived His
human life. This is a pity; and though the consideration of the life of our

soul passionately desires that its life should be in perfect harmony with that life of which Christ, its Head, has the plenitude. It is perfectly aware that it cannot receive the inflow of that life to the fullest of its own capacity, unless there disappears from it all pulsations of the life of self which in its tendencies is opposed to the spirit of the life of Christ. Its object now is to check all unsupernatural movements in itself, in order that its whole life may be supernaturalised and that thus it may be brought into perfect union with Jesus Christ Himself.

All manifestations of the inordinate life of self become abhorrent to it for the sole reason that they prevent the perfection of that union and harmony between itself, as member, and the Head of that Mystical Body. In other words, the soul wishes to become a healthy cell in the Mystical Body of Christ, a cell fully vivified by the life that animates that Body ; it shrinks from the condition of being a languishing one, possessing only a tainted or incomplete life.

Lord is never without benefit, the lack of some definite method of approach may explain much " flabby " spirituality among holy persons, and some absence of progress in the spiritual life.

As a matter of fact, the human life of our Lord is dominated by one fundamental principle, namely, the complete and entire subjection of His human will to the Divine Will of His heavenly Father. He came not to do His own will but the will of Him that sent Him. (cf. St. John vi. 38.) His prayer in the garden was one of complete submission to His Father, " Not my will but thine be done ", (St. Luke xxii. 42), and His whole life has been told by St. Paul in one short phrase, " He was made obedient even unto death ". (Phil. ii. 8.) If His life was marked by the virile acceptance of suffering, obscurity and poverty, it is because He would teach us that by the willing acceptance of these things from the hand of God, we too can most easily overcome the attractions which earth holds out to self-love, in order to base our lives on the fundamental principle of His life—that of loving subjection to God—and so by impregnating our lives with the spirit of His, become in very truth " other Christs " (cf. Marmion : Christ the Life of the Soul, chap. ii, especially the concluding paragraphs).

Venial sins weaken the vital energy of the Body; they diminish the fervour of charity and impoverish grace which is as it were, the soul of the Mystical Body of Christ.[6] The conscience, therefore, becomes very delicate and shrinks from everything that falls short of a complete conformity to the will of God. Deviation from that will, even when far short of opposition to it, appears in its real horror. It has to do extreme violence to all its newborn instincts to commit a single deliberate fault; and if it falls into such, it is seized with a lively and keen remorse. Its infidelities become rarer, at least deliberate infidelities —though the soul is still weak and can fail frequently through frailty. But it cannot for a moment leave go of God to attach itself to something else—even though that attachment may not be positively displeasing to God—without instantly hearing His reproach in the depths of its interior. The Lord's voice makes itself heard reproachfully at every infidelity.[7] The soul grows rapidly in purity of conscience, and its confessions become very sincere; its faults are traced back with perfect surety of discernment to their true source, which is always a want of correspondence in some direction or other to God's designs of love. It has a growing discernment of the action of God

---

[6] Cf. Van Noort. *De Ecclesia Christi* § 74, "Sanctifying grace is rightly called the soul of the Church".

[7] The relations between Christ and the soul at this stage are aptly expressed by *The Imitation*, Book III, xxxii, in the colloquy :—

"*Christ*—Take this short and perfect word : Forsake all and thou shalt find all, leave thy desires and thou shalt find rest.

Disciple—Lord this is not the work of one day, nor children's sport.

Christ—When thou art come so far that thou art no longer a lover of thyself, but dost stand wholly at my beck . . . then wouldst thou exceedingly please me and all thy life would pass in joy and peace ".

on it, and understands to a large extent how it can in its own activities co-operate with or impede that action. It now perceives how its every act has an effect on its own state, and makes for or mars its growth in supernatural life.

Its contrition is deeper and more perfect, though all traces of irritation and bitterness against self have disappeared from its sorrow for sin. It abhors its faults now not as being a humiliating reminder of its native weakness and imperfection, nor yet because of the loss and harm of which they are the cause, but simply because they render it less apt to serve God's purposes. Its sorrow is all for God and not for self; it views these faults in His light not in its own, and therefore sees them justly and truly; it sees them not only in themselves, but in their sources. The purpose of amendment is directed to more than the elimination of the actual sins; it aims at the mortifying of the principle from which they spring. The examination of conscience is no longer a mere enquiry into the nature and number of its faults; it is no longer a mere review of the " facts " of its spiritual existence; it has become a study of the relations, in which the soul stands to Almighty God, of the measure of its want of correspondence to His grace, and finally of the obstacles it opposes by its imperfections to the accomplishment of the Divine will in its regard.

The particular kind of life the soul is leading, will naturally determine the direction which its positive activity towards spiritual progress will take. Having only one purpose in view and that the promotion of God's glory, it will have only one object to tend towards and that is to extirpate in itself all that prevents God's glory being realised through its instrumentality. If the soul has adopted the contemplative life as its vocation, it will aim at consoling the Lord by its fidelity, by its delicate attentions to Him and by the warmth of its affection, for the abandonment He suffers from others. The soul desires that it should be a holy place where the Lord may come to take His rest, and where He may find nothing but profound adoration, deep sympathy and warm affection. It aims at excluding everything from its way of acting that could displease the Lord or render His presence less intimate. Dissipation, purely natural activity, or want of fervour are the kind of faults that frustrate the realisation of the glory God is to gain through that soul, and the soul reproaches itself with deep sorrow if it has been betrayed by its frailty into any faults. Inevitably in its conversations with God it will gravitate towards this ruling thought—now become the Christian motive of its life—that of lending itself to be a perfect and willing instrument in the hands of God, for the fulfilment of His designs. The petition of its prayer will be for fervour, recollection and interior peace, as being the means which will render it pliable under the action of the Holy Ghost.

If devoted to the active or apostolic life, its energy will be directed to the correction of those faults and defects of temperament or character which might hamper its action on souls and check the flow of the Divine influence which Jesus wills to transmit through it to others. Therefore in order to have more power to attract souls, it will with an eagerness inspired by love, work hard to bring under control all movements of impatience, rigidity and uncharitableness. On account of its high ideals—which it believes only too low—it will at first tend to be hard and exacting with weak and cowardly souls that choose to move in a lower plane than itself. But the Lord Who does not " break the bruised reed and extinguish the smoking flax ", reveals to it that such a hard and exacting spirit is not His. It sees in this illumination that it must cultivate a Divine tolerance of weakness in others, and cultivate in itself a peace so solidly established that it cannot be disturbed by the ceaseless difficulties that God's work encounters in this world. This tolerance of weakness in others combined with an intolerance of what is in any way wrong, and this peace of soul which should remain unshaken by any manifestation of wickedness, are necessary, it realises, for the full exercise on the souls of others of the supernatural vigour which the soul itself possesses. It will naturally make all its conversations with Jesus converge on the acquisition of the qualities which were so perfectly exemplified in Our Blessed Saviour's apostolic dealings with men, namely, gentleness to sinners, intolerance of sin and calm of soul. These apostolic motives will furnish the theme of all its petitions.

In this connection it is not out of place to deal with the Particular Examen, an exercise which presents a considerable amount of difficulty to the best intentioned soul ; but one which can become, instead of a distasteful duty a most consoling and fruitful spiritual occupation. There should be no rigid line of demarcation between the Meditation and the Particular Examen.

The latter should be the taking up or the resumption, under a particular aspect, of the former. The stage of prayer should always determine the subject of the Examination; in the first stage it will be some glaring defect, the cause of frequent falls—for instance, luke-warmness, sloth, sensuality, carelessness of rule, a habit of criticism or the like; in the second stage, the reproaches of the conscience will turn on self-seeking in one or other of its various forms, inordinate affections, want of kindness to others, eagerness for our own perfection and the like; in the third stage the examination will turn on that particular thing in us which we find to be a hindrance to the free intercourse of the Lord with our souls. Instances of those obstacles have already been cited; they are want of sincerity, or of simplicity, a tendency to irritation against wrong doing, a habit of exaggeration, hastiness in speech and in action, a yielding to weakness in handling the affairs of the Lord, failure in meekness or patience, and other faults of this kind. The soul casts a rapid glance over the twenty-four hours to see if it has fallen and how many times into the particular fault to which it is prone; it reviews the occasions in which these faults have occurred, with a view to taking precautions in similar circumstances the next time, and it strives to trace the different faults it discovers back to some single fundamental defect in itself. This review should be rapid and never exceed a few minutes. The soul then excites itself to a sincere regret for what it has done, and this it will do without difficulty because it sees in all its faults an impediment to its own movement under the high motive by which its life is directed. When after the expression of its sorrow it has made a humble petition for help in its future trials it will tranquilly resume the spiritual position it occupied with the Lord at the termination of the morning's mental prayer.[8]

As the soul subjects itself more and more to the Divine Master's influences and enters ever further into His views, its devotions undergo an important change; they become less and less the expression of a human spirit and more and more the expression of a divine: "Likewise, the Spirit also helpeth our infirmity. For we know not what we should pray for as we ought; but the Spirit himself asketh for us with unspeakable groanings ".[9] The liturgical prayers commence to exercise a powerful attraction over it; they begin to lay bare to its vision their beauty, and to its understanding their hidden depths of meaning. It enters more fully and completely into the life of the Church, and begins to think and feel with the Spouse of Christ. The movements of grace forthwith in the soul correspond with the movement of the liturgical life. It is given to the soul to enter into, and to participate in, the different mysteries of the Saviour's life, as if it were itself a personal actor in those events; and it derives from these mysteries, as unfolded and developed in the Liturgical Cycle,

---

[8] But the Particular Examen is not always necessarily directed towards the correction of faults and in the later stages is particularly effective in producing a positive result. It may be used with great efficacy to form, e.g., a habit of prayer, of self-abandonment, of supernatural living (i.e., of accepting events in the spirit of faith), or of conscious advertence to the presence of God in the soul—all of which habits are direct and ideal preparations for union.

[9] Rom. viii. 26.

the particular graces of sanctification which they are
ordained to impart. The feasts of the Church become
for it spiritual feasts which fill it with grace and joy,
making its prayer merge naturally into the sentiments
which animate the Church on these occasions, and
to which utterance is given in the Office and in the
Mass. The soul begins to respond to every movement
which vibrates in the Church. Its life becomes mystic
in increasing measure, for its whole natural existence—
namely the daily round of human duties—tends to
be lifted into a supernatural plane by the close union
with Christ's life on earth that has been developed.
Things which before cost bitter struggles now become
easy to it. Asceticism no longer costs an effort. It
is no longer a rude self-discipline to bring the soul
into subjection to Christ. This subjection now follows
as a natural consequence from the merging of the
soul's life in that of Christ and from the soul's ardent
desire to live in constant fidelity to the promptings
of the Holy Spirit. The soul now attains to God's
view-point with regard to life's events; it sees them
as He sees them, and in the perspective in which He
views them. The absolute futility of the things of
earth is revealed in a strong and vivid light, and in
a vigorous contrast with the reality that is God, and
with all that pertains to Him and His service. Through
the activity of the gift of Wisdom, creatures are
seen in the light of their First Cause and thus seen
in their emptiness and vanity they cease to exercise
any attraction over the soul. They no longer hold
it, but it holds them, for it has risen above and
established itself in the source of all created things,

" Blessed are the poor in spirit for theirs is the Kingdom of Heaven ",[10] its perfect detachment has won for it the reward promised in this beatitude. Having renounced earth, it has found God and in Him it has recovered creatures once again. They become of interest to it, but to the extent only in which it sees God in them. Creatures have not only lost the power to attract; they have lost also the faculty to wound. Things that hurt before, can still strike but they cannot move, for the soul remains unaffected by anything that touches itself personally.[11] Having merged its individuality in that of the Church, it can be wounded only through the latter. Its interests and ambitions being bound up with hers, its only pursuit being the extension and the building of the body of Christ, it is only the malice or the wickedness that opposes an obstacle to this end, that can cause it pain. It is only what hurts the Church can hurt it. Hence it feels a passionate hatred of error, of false teaching, of false principles, of worldly maxims, and of every invention of Satan by which souls are corrupted and destroyed. It can enter into wrath about these things, for it is yet imperfect and has not attained to that higher calm, where it enters into the unruffled tranquillity of God.

[10] St. Matt. v. 3. The present tense is significant.
[11] This does not mean that the sensitive nature is atrophied or deadened. It is so controlled and influenced by the will divinely illumined that it ceases to clamour for recognition or alleviation. As a matter of fact extreme sensitiveness to pain inflicted by creatures frequently seems to co-exist with, and be a very accompaniment of, an intense love of God. Love for God does not encase the human heart with a crust as it were, making it invulnerable to hurt inflicted by creatures, but it so mingles its divine balm with poor human sensitiveness, and so enlightens, sustains and directs the will, that the soul is not disturbed, and finds even a deeper peace. (Sensitiveness to pain is a powerful help for developing growth in union with God.)

This calm it can enjoy only in the realm of Passive Prayer.

The soul holding itself detached from creatures, can easily supernaturalise its work, for it has become habitual to regard everything it has to do as being appointed to it by God Himself. The commonest things thus become of value, and cease at the same time to have any value in its eyes—a strange paradox, one of the many with which the whole Christian life is interwoven, all being based upon the fundamental one of life through death and death in life. Things are of value because they are God's appointment; they cease to have value because they are regarded as being nothing in themselves, and as having only the worth that that appointment of God gives them. Hence the soul relinquishes its tasks easily as soon as obedience calls it to some other charge. No longer seeking itself, but God in those things, it leaves off as soon as God can no longer be found in them; and it knows well that God can be found in occupations only as long as duty or authority binds it to them. In a word, the soul lives and moves and breathes in a completely supernatural atmosphere; out of it, it feels restless, unhappy and ill at ease; it views itself and all things else from the vantage ground of heaven; the supernatural has become for it quasi-natural. Its prayer, without deliberate intention, tends to simplify itself more and more. Having learned by experience the poverty of the results that attend on its own eager activities, and on the other hand the strengthening and transforming effect of the least action of God, it contents itself with putting itself in the Divine

Presence and willing to submit itself to the Divine influence. It knows full well that its best activity is to hold itself in that attitude which disposes it to receive from the hand of God the gifts of God. The soul is well advised in giving itself to this form of prayer when grace draws it to this manner of treating with God. " For the soul is, in the last resort, but a mere capacity. It has nothing from itself and in itself. It is on God it must draw to fill up the void, and this it does by the union with Him developed in prayer. It ought, therefore, rather receive than take. Consequently the perfect state of prayer consists in this, that the faculties of the soul are united in a contemplation marked by silence, calm and expectancy. This being so, the soul's co-operation (in the work of sanctification) consists in consenting to the gifts of God and in receiving them. . . . This silence and this expectancy of the soul before God must constitute a state of dependence on the Author of all gifts, of annihilation before Him and of adoration of His greatness."[12]

This state of the soul, excellent as it is, is not without its own dangers. The process of purification is not yet complete and that being so, there remains the possibility of lapses into serious and even grave faults. This danger diminishes considerably—only in rare cases does it altogether disappear—when passive prayer begins. In the most perfect form of the prayer of simplicity, such as has been described, the soul is still only at the threshold of that life of comparative security ; to cross that threshold it must

[12] Ven. Libermann : *Ecrits Spirituels* p. 217.

practise the utmost fidelity in the details of life. It is only this constant and sustained and minute fidelity to the touches of grace that will make it pass into the stages of passive prayer. Its prayer at the point at which it has arrived is in its highest expression the prayer of simplicity. This is still active prayer, though the activity is largely of the will ; the operations of the intelligence are few and simple ; they no longer involve reasoning and discourse ; they consist mainly in a peaceful regard, which embraces in a single intuition all the aspects of the subject meditated on and its consequences. Very frequently at this point of spiritual progress the soul undergoes an experience which causes it, if uninstructed, a great deal of anxiety and misgiving. Prayer has become easy. Entering into contact with God presents little difficulty. The mind readily turns to Divine things and the will is easily stirred up to affection for them. Everything seems to point to a rapid and indefinite progress in the practice of prayer, when suddenly or slowly the soul finds all its hopes, to all appearances, shattered. When it places itself before God for its daily exercise of mental prayer it finds itself, as it appears to it, utterly unable to pray. The understanding is apparently sluggish and inert. There seems to be no vital reaction on the part of the intelligence to the ' points ' that the devout soul prepares for its meditation. Consideration after consideration is suggested and they rest on the surface of the mind lifeless, like stones on the surface of a frozen lake. They seem not to penetrate the mind, to become part of it and to issue in further reflections or in affections of the will. There is as

little response from the mind as there would be on
the part of an inanimate body to a stimulus applied
to it. The soul feels, as it were, paralysed.

The time of prayer, owing to the apparent inability
of the understanding to work, is filled with distractions.
The soul is tempted to believe that it is a waste of
precious moments, has no useful effect and only excites
the displeasure of God. It is tempted to renounce
the formal exercise of mental prayer as useless and
unprofitable. The temptation is all the stronger because it finds that outside the time of formal prayer,
during the occupations of the day, in difficulties, in
labours, in joyous incidents, it finds a comparative
ease in raising itself to God in aspirations and
affections.

Another troubling phenomenon accompanying this
species of seeming paralysis in prayer is the loss of
taste for spiritual reading. Up to this juncture the
soul found keen delight in perusing the works of
ascetical and spiritual writers. Their thoughts nourished
it, illuminated the understanding, stirred up the desire
for Divine things and ministered ample matter for the
exercise of the mind during the times of prayer. Now
it reads and gets nothing from the reading. Whole
paragraphs are gone through and no savour is found
in them. The books have become to the understanding
as food that has lost its savour and all its nutritious
properties. If the soul holds on to its spiritual
reading (as of course, it should) it does so in a
sense of duty and it acquits itself of it as of a task—
a task that seems to have little practical value or
significance.

The soul sees in all this, clear signs of its having gone backwards and is naturally troubled thereat. But it can console itself, for all these symptoms are not signs of retrogression *if deliberate faults have been avoided and if the practices of the spiritual life have been clung to.*[13] The explanation of this peculiar and fearful state of soul is found in the very progress that the soul has made. Up to this point there has been a gradual forming of convictions with regard to the principles of perfection and a steady approach on the part of the will to that point at which its affections are definitely weaned from all that is not God or does not lead to Him. The result is that all efforts at thinking itself into this condition—which is the normal purpose of meditation—are wasted efforts and issue in a sense of futility. It is a veritable " carrying of coals to Newcastle " in the realm of spiritual things.

This explains the irritation of the soul when it strives to carry on its exercise as usual. If it were enlightened enough at the moment it would understand that the impatience at the usual procedure of turning over points of considerations, is due to an inner consciousness that this process has become a veritable distraction turning it aside from something more profitable. The soul has no longer need to form convictions. It is penetrated through and through with the sense of

---

[13] The aridity in prayer which is treated of here is not the same as that mentioned in Ch. vi., though analogous to it. The trial spoken of in the present Chapter always presupposes a period of marked spiritual advancement. On the other hand, the trial described in Ch. vi. is essentially that which besets a beginner when God deprives the soul of sensible delights in prayer either to lead it in the obscurity of faith to solid virtue, or to warn it of some negligence in His service.

the desirability of God. This anxiety to grow closer
to God, to know Him more and to love Him more
meets with very little resistance now; it meets with
none when the soul finds itself in the presence of God
for prayer. The instinct of the soul at this point, if
the instinct is not thwarted through a wrong understanding of things, is to content itself with dwelling
quietly in spirit before God, with a single expectant
look towards Him and without any multiplicity of
acts either of will or intellect. It has reached a
stage when it has, so to speak, developed a
decided taste for God and can relish little else. It
has no need to persuade itself to this taste any
longer. Hence considerations weary it and prove
distasteful.

Of course, owing to the fewness and simplicity
of the acts of the intelligence, the imagination is apt
to run riot. Distractions are numerous and even dis-
quieting. But the soul need not be disturbed, for
underneath the rippling of these distractions over the
surface of the soul, the soul, in its depths, is adhering
to God in a sustained act of loving regard. In spite
of the wanderings of the imagination the will is adhering
to God and the understanding is dwelling on Him.

The difficulty presented by spiritual reading is simply
another aspect of the difficulty in considerations. The
soul has learned all about the principles and practice
of the interior life. It has nothing more to get from
books. These fail to present it with any further stimulus
to a cult of spirituality. The period of forming convictions and acquiring ideas is over and past. The time
has not yet come when the soul is so advanced that

a paragraph or even a sentence from the most common-place spiritual book can illuminate the understanding in a fresh and vivid way and stir up the affections to warmth. A most ordinary word about God suffices to set perfect souls aflame. But that stage is not yet reached. The soul must therefore expectantly keep itself in peace, and in the meantime choose for its spiritual reading those books which have a peculiar unction; the Holy Scriptures, the *Imitation of Christ*, the works of the great Saints and Doctors of the Church.

Trials such as these should remind the soul that the virtues are still in their tenderest growth, and constant watchfulness is necessary to prevent this growth from being checked or destroyed. But the great danger of the soul comes from the temptation which is peculiar to the state in which it finds itself. It has surmounted sensuality; it has emancipated itself from the love of creatures; but it still can be ensnared by the innate, instinctive and humanly speaking, ineradicable " appetite "[14] to be something. This tendency can be described better in negative than in positive terms. There is in every person a shrinking from what may be described as ' moral eclipse '. It is a shuddering fear of annihilation in a moral not physical sense. It is a shrinking from obscurity and oblivion. It is a dread of being counted by men as being nothing and as not to be taken account of at

[14] The scholastic word ' appetite '—derived from ' ad ', to, and ' petere ', to seek—is chosen deliberately as the only term suited to convey the idea that is meant to be expressed. Anxiety, desire, wish, ambition—these words are too strong, as they imply something that is too positive and deliberate. What is designated by the word ' appetite ' is more like an instinct—the instinct proper to and springing from personality.

all. To be despised, and what is worse, to be unknown, to be forgotten, to be buried in obscurity as far as regards one's fellow-creatures, that is extremely hard for human nature to bear, and human nature, even much chastened, shrinks back from it. Even one who is exercised in virtue will still retain this "appetite" to be something. This appetite can be free from the taint of ambition, vanity and selfishness. It may be free from all self-seeking in the vulgar sense. It springs not from the instinct of self-seeking, but from what may be called the instinct of self-preservation, understanding this term in its most transcendental sense in the moral order. One swayed by this "appetite" may desire "to be something" in view of the interests of God. Such a one, ardently desirous of doing something for God, of spending Himself in His service and of winning souls to Him, may judge that in order to succeed in this it would be necessary for it to be well thought of and to be held in a certain amount of esteem. Without exactly seeking to acquire a reputation for the possession of excellent qualities, a virtuous soul may not be unwilling that it should appear to others to be in possession of these qualities in order that they, submitting to its ascendency, may be in this way led to God.

This corresponds to the third temptation. The devil suggested to Our Lord that He should do some striking thing in the eyes of men, insinuating that they would thereby be more ready to be swayed by His words and to be persuaded to follow His teaching; "And he brought Him to Jerusalem, and he set Him on a pinnacle of the temple, and he said to Him; if

thou be the Son of God, cast thyself from hence. For
it is written, that He hath given His angels charge
over thee, that they keep thee. And that in their hands
they shall bear thee up lest perhaps thou dash thy
foot against a stone ".[15] The reasoning implicit in
this suggestion is very specious. " You are unknown
and obscure ; as such you will get no hearing with
the people and your enterprise will meet with no
success. Do something striking, show yourself to
be somebody and the people will acknowledge you
as the Messias." The reply of Jesus was simple :
" Thou shalt not tempt the Lord thy God ". That is
to say, " I leave the manifestation of what I am to
God to be made according to His good pleasure and
at the time and in the circumstances He determines ".
Christ refuses to anticipate the time and the action
of God by putting Himself forward of His own accord.
So too, must we be disposed to remain hidden, obscure
and unknown to men, if God so wills it. If He chooses
to manifest His power through us, He must be left
His own time to do so. God fulfils Himself in many
ways, and we can never know whether He shall realise
His purpose in us through keeping us hidden or
bringing us into the light. The soul that seeks to be
perfect must consent to be nothing, that is, to be held
as nobody. It is wrong to seek to do remarkable things
in God's service for the sake of attracting others to
that service. Self would be sure to recover itself in
that.[16]

[15] St. Luke iv. 9–11.

[16] It is noteworthy that as the soul progresses in prayer and in the interior
life, temptations become more subtle and insidious and in a sense more
terrifying in their nature. The soul is not any longer set in opposition to

This temptation can be extraordinarily subtle, and it must be the sharpest one in the devil's armoury for it is the only one of the three that he renews with Our Lord. " And his brethren said to Him; Pass from hence and go into Judea; that thy disciples also may see thy works which thou dost. For there is no man that doth anything in secret, and he himself seeketh to be known openly. If thou do these things manifest thyself to the world."[17] This is the same temptation in another form; Jesus is told by His brethren that He can conquer hearts and wills, by an exhibition of the power of which He is possessed —" show yourself to be somebody and a career awaits you ". The Evangelist adds with a certain sadness and pathos, " For neither did his brethren believe in Him ".[18] They could not see with His eyes; they saw only through the eyes of the world—the world which judges self-advertisement to be a necessary means to success. With a strange persistency the devil returned once more with the same suggestion during Our Lord's last moments; this time it came through the scribes and ancients of the people—

God by the attraction of creatures—it feels itself set in opposition to God because of Himself. It begins to experience a species of resentment against God Himself, which appals it because of the fearful wickedness of the temptation. It feels in itself a dislike of the Divinity itself and a distaste for God and a tendency to blasphemy and hatred. The reason lies in this. The soul has, in its progress, penetrated very far into its own interior and is now having a practical experimentation of the fundamental opposition between self and God. Self is driven to its last stronghold and resents God with all its spiritual energy. The soul must not be terrified at this experience. It is a sign of the nearness, not the remoteness of God. It must be quietly and wisely alert to these snares of self-love and of the wicked one. It must trust in God to enlighten it and to direct the work of uprooting the clinging " self " which would impede the perfect union with Him.

[17] St. John vii. 3–4.
[18] John vii. 5.

" Mocking, they said, if he be the king of Israel, let him now come down from the cross and we will believe him ".[19] By an appeal to the Divine Power that was His in virtue of the Hypostatic Union, Jesus could detach Himself from the cross; if He made such an appeal and did come down, perhaps the incredulity of His enemies would be overcome? Such was the temptation. Jesus paid no heed to the tempter. He consented to appear there before the whole world completely helpless, wholly powerless and an abject failure. He consented to appear there on the cross as the " Most abject of men ",[20] as a very nothing from the points of human dignity and worth. His attitude was the complete negation of that tendency in man " to be something ":—" There is no beauty in him . . . whereupon we esteemed him not ",[21] He is " a worm and no man, the reproach of men and the outcast of the people".[22] And yet it was this utter annihilation in all human estimation that wrought the redemption of mankind. There was no failure like Christ's, and yet it was the world's salvation; so too from the bruised and crushed human soul God can draw an immense flood of spiritual energy for the regeneration of mankind, provided that the soul does not allow itself to break and lose heart and courage under its cruel suffering. When the soul, in its earnest pursuit of God has allowed this last citadel in it to yield to grace, the citadel of that pride by which a man obstinately resists being nothing in the eyes of men—when it has attained this degree of humility,

---

[19] St. Matt. xxvii. 42.
[20] Isaias liii. 3.
[21] Isaias liii. 2, 3.
[22] Ps. xxi. 7.

then it is perfectly prepared for that direct divine action on it, which prepares the way for close, intimate and habitual union with God.

Union with God is effected by the action of the three faculties of understanding, memory, and will, operating through the divine infused virtues of faith, hope and charity. It is the activity of those virtues that attaches the soul to its Creator, as its final end. In the degree in which this activity is intense and unintermittent, the union is intimate and unbroken. The obstacle to the free action of the infused virtues of faith, hope and charity in the soul is the activity of the three concupiscences, the concupiscence of the flesh, the concupiscence of the eyes, and the pride of life—the sad heritage of original sin. By these concupiscences man is attached to himself, to his bodily pleasures, to what gratifies his imagination, and to what flatters his intellect and will. Attached to himself by the activities of the concupiscences, he is necessarily detached from God. In the preceding chapters has been sketched the series of efforts the soul has to make to vanquish its sensuality, its affections and its pride, and by these victories to paralyse the activities of the concupiscences. When these enemies are overcome, the soul finds itself unhampered and unimpeded in the exercise of the theological virtues of Faith, Hope and Charity. This free and unfettered action of the infused virtues is called the perfect spiritual life. " It is called spiritual," writes Ven. Libermann " because in it the soul detaches itself and withdraws from every material object to apply itself to God alone and to spiritual things ; it makes of this its whole life. It no longer allows itself to be dominated or impressed by sensible objects, but by God alone with whom it is in intimate relation. It no longer lives save to serve God in spirit and truth. Its life is a life of religion."[23]

[23] Ven. Libermann : *Ecrits Spirituels*, p. 9.

CHAPTER IX

" And after six days Jesus taketh with Him Peter and James and John and leadeth them up into an high mountain apart by themselves and was transfigured before them." Mark ix. 1, Luke ix. 28, Matt. xvii. 1.

IN the instructions on the interior life, the growth of the soul seems to have been described solely as a progress in dispossession of self. Though purporting to be the science of the development of life, mental prayer has apparently as its term and its achievement nothing else than the complete death of self. The different stages of advancement through which the soul passes were shown to be processes of self-renouncement carried to an ever higher degree of perfection, and penetrating ever more profoundly to the depths of our nature. Now this result, however much to be desired, is merely negative, and considering what it costs, in the way of suffering and mortification, it, in itself, holds out no attraction to warm our imagination ; it is too chilling an ideal to sustain our courage in the real hardship that the spiritual combat involves. To very many the way of the interior life will appear in this light only. Spirituality will mean the mere negation of nature. The election of super- natural life will be regarded as the renouncement of all joy and happiness. What is more the soul, not understanding any pleasure except that which is derived through the satisfaction of natural tastes, desires and impulses, is persuaded that once it leaves these, it has to abandon delectation in every form. It does not see and cannot realise that delectation can exist under other forms. The invitation to enter into the spiritual life, is, it believes, an invitation to enter into a region from which is shut out all light and heat, and which is chill with the chillness of the grave. Growth in spirituality seems to be a process of death, which at best, issues in an existence vague, shadowy and intangible —holding out nothing to which our poor nature can cling and in which it can find its rest. The life of prayer thus envisaged, is harsh and forbidding, and it is not surprising that many, understanding it in this manner only, shrink from entering upon it, or, if they have made a beginning relinquish the undertaking at the first strong appeal of nature. The life of prayer was expected to be a growth in intimacy with Jesus and, for those whose courage has not carried them beyond the preliminary stages, it has turned out to be a disheartening revelation of self.

It is not correct to regard mental prayer at any of its stages as a mere process of self-revelation and self-emptying. It is true that, in the description of the gradual perfecting of the soul, a great deal of stress was laid upon the question of the abnegation that conditions this perfection. But there never was an instant in which this abnegation constituted the totality of the soul process. Side by side with the negative movement there went a positive; the relinquishing of oneself was accompanied by the attainment of something infinitely better. There was a passage from nothingness to reality—from darkness to light. In the beginning our vision of the supernatural is almost

totally, though not quite, obscured by the presence
of the natural. Our soul is enveloped in a mist. The
process of self-renouncement is the gradual removal
of this curtain of darkness, and as this process proceeds
our intuition of the things of God becomes clearer.
These are revealed to us in the humanity of Jesus
Christ. True self-revelation has always as its counter-
part a growth in knowledge of God. For it is only
in the light of God that we see ourselves for what we
are. Hence self-abnegation in its full import is not
a merely negative thing; as self in its destruction
disappears from our view the vision of Our Divine
Lord takes its place. According as the soul ceases
to be "*self-regarding*" in its activities, it becomes
"*God-regarding*". As the soul is being emptied of
what is material, transient and perishable, it is being
filled with what is spiritual, enduring and incorruptible:

The soul in itself is, as it were, a void—but an
infinite one. It is a capacity for the unlimited. Its
characteristic actuality is a yearning and a longing for
satisfaction that nothing finite can gratify. Having no
resources of its own on which to draw, it cannot find
in itself what will supply its native nothingness. It is,
therefore, obliged to reach out, to seize something
external to itself, in order to satisfy its needs. It is
an infinite potentiality. This explains the restlessness
and dissatisfaction that all men experience—and from
which the saints even, to a certain degree, are not
exempt; though, in them, it is found conjoined, as
will be seen later, with a certain tranquillising of their
longings. But the majority of people carried away by
the attraction that pleasure exercises over their senses,

give themselves up to the pursuit of exterior things, in order to appease the soul's desires. Each pleasant object holds out a promise of satisfying the soul's aspirations; but it is found incapable of bringing to an end the restless striving of the soul to complete itself. Satisfaction after satisfaction is sought; one object after another is added to one's possessions, and yet one finds oneself still with that awful feeling of emptiness of being with which all those who do not seek God are familiar.

And this must necessarily be so. The capacity of the soul cannot be filled up except by what can be received into it; and, by sensible satisfaction, we can reach only the surface of any created thing. No matter how close to ourselves we may hold it, no matter how intimate the possession, if created, it still remains outside of us and in purely external contact. The soul remains in its emptiness and with its restlessness unsatisfied,— its groping after completeness fruitless. Its thirst after fulness of being, remains unslaked—" Whosoever drinketh of this water shall thirst again ", says Jesus.[1] The water to which Our Lord makes allusion is created satisfaction in any form whatsoever—it is the whole universe of created things considered as the source of natural delectation. No matter how good these satisfactions may be in themselves, they cannot be our entire and final good, for they cannot complete our being. To do this it would be necessary for them to be capable of being drawn into our souls and united with them,—to become as it were the soul's substance, much as food is transformed into the substance of the

[1] St. John iv. 13.

body. To realise this affective identification is the aim
of all affection and the pain of love consists precisely
in the futility of the effort. This is illustrated in the
purest of all human affections, that of a mother for her
child. Love always tends to union—and pure love to
the surrender to, and union of oneself with the person
loved. When the mother strains the child to her bosom,
there is in that a passionate desire that their two beings
should be fused into one. This desire is ever to be
thwarted. The contact though so close, so intimate,
still remains an external one—one soul cannot be fused
with the other. And this is true, in its own measure, of
every affection ; we shall find, if we analyse our feelings,
that in every case where we pursue or cherish any
created being, there is on our part a longing to be one
with that object ; and the more we love, the more
ardent is our desire to identify ourselves in taste, in
thought, in feeling with the cherished creature. What
is more, this striving goes further, it tends towards and
aims at identification in being in as far as that is possible.
And of course this aim is always thwarted ; hence it
is that every created affection even though legitimate
is attended by pain. The only thing that could ease
that pain, would be the physical possession by the
soul of the creature loved. But this cannot be. Hence
it is that even though one should accumulate around
oneself all the treasures that have come from the hand
of God, even though one should taste to the full all
the satisfaction that creation is capable of yielding,
still, after all that, nothing has really entered into the
soul, it still remains in its original state of void—of
mere capacity that has not been filled—still a prey to

the tortures of infinite yearnings, which have in no way been appeased.

Nothing can fill up the infinite capacity in the human soul except what can physically enter into it and take possession of it—and this privilege belongs to the Creator alone, and to that participation of His life which is given in grace and in glory. "Thou hast made us for Thee, O Lord, and our hearts are restless till they rest in Thee," says St. Augustine. Nothing but God and the life of God can enter into the human soul, and therefore, nothing but God can still its restlessness. And though nothing but the complete possession of God (received in the life after death) can fill to the full the measure of its capacity and reduce its strivings to perfect repose, still, the slightest degree of union with the Divinity, gives a degree of satisfaction directly proportionate to the measure of that union—a satisfaction that infinitely surpasses all that could be ministered by the whole created universe. The reason is that God is in the soul, and created things are not; by union with God something is added to the soul, by earthly pleasures, nothing; by the smallest degree of spiritual happiness is given some actuality, whereas, by the highest measure of created satisfaction, is given but the appearance of reality. "But he that shall drink of the water that I will give him," says Our Lord, "shall not thirst for ever."[2]

It is true that the soul shall always feel a longing to enter more and more into the possession of God— or rather to be more and more possessed by God— and this longing is a kind of thirst. But still it is thirst

[2] St. John iv. 13.

that is being ever satisfied, and as such, is a pleasure
rather than a pain. Love, as was said, ever desires
union. This is even more true of spiritual than of
earthly love. The soul that "is taken with God"
ardently desires to be, as it were, one with Him, longs
that God should enter more fully into itself, and begs
with earnest prayers, that He should take more complete possession of it. As regards its own disposition,
it looks for one thing only, namely that everything in
itself that prevents the completeness of this possession
of itself by God should disappear, and labours, therefore,
with extraordinary earnestness to make to vanish the
last vestiges of its own independent life, in order to
throb only with the life of God. Its striving is never
destined to cease until its every movement is a response
to the Divine impulses; until is attained that perfect
union which is the very one-ness dreamed of by love
in its highest expression.

Yet, still, although the soul in this world, even
in its spiritual life, is never at rest, it is never restless; though it is never satisfied it is never dissatisfied;
though it is never without movement it is never
troubled: because, at each moment it is attaining
some degree of that "Reality" for which it is created.
Until it has completely drunk into itself God, its thirst
is not perfectly slaked, but with each degree of God's
life that is taken into it, it is satisfying that thirst.
Hence it is that the possession of God granted us in
this world gives happiness—and our want of possession
of Him gives a happiness too, for spiritual delights
once tasted both satisfy the appetite and create an
appetite for more. The longing for them by one who

has experienced them is a happiness in itself.[3] The Saints speak of the delights of the pain of longing for that degree of union with God not yet attained.

And this happiness is the state towards which mental prayer of itself tends. It is not the end at which we should aim in entering on the interior life. For we must be careful to seek God alone and not the happiness that is found in His service, and be ever ready to seek Him though this pursuit be attended with pain and aridity. But in fact the happiness referred to is always found conjoined with the cultivation of the interior life—and is its connatural term.

We are created to know God with a supernatural knowledge. This supernatural knowledge of God implies a knowledge of God as He is in Himself—by faith in this life and by the light of glory in the next. Further supernatural intellectual knowledge through faith that worketh by charity implies possession, in this case not mere representative possession but physical possession. For God the Holy Spirit has *His Habitation* in the souls of the just, and this habitation means presence not in the ideal but in the real manner. When faith is animated by charity God is held and possessed by the soul in the very substantiality of His being. It is true that the intellect operating through faith sees Him only by means of ideas derived from created things. Its knowledge in this life remains always of the abstractive kind. The intellect as yet cannot have an idea which adequately manifests God to it. But nevertheless it is God Himself that it is contemplating

[3] Cf. Homily of St. Gregory in the Gospel of the Sunday within the Octave of Corpus Christi.

in such ideas of divine things as it is capable of forming under the light of faith and theology. But dim and obscure and imperfect as is this abstractive knowledge of God it gives to the prayerful soul a deep contentment, a profound peace, and a tranquil satisfaction. The soul is knowing God to some extent and it knows too that it possesses in itself, in the reality of His Divine Being, the object which it is knowing. Even in the natural order our purest pleasure is derived from intellectual insight. When the mind has at last seen light on some problem that perplexed it, when its doubts and hesitations disappear as the shadows before an illumination, there is felt a kind of exaltation which carries with it the keenest satisfaction. We are said to grasp, to hold, to possess the truth. The object itself does not become intimate to us, but its ideal representation. We possess not the object itself, but an idea of it,[4] and yet this shadowy possession is capable of giving deepest pleasure. How much greater is the contentment that is experienced by the interior soul as it knows that in apprehending God by faith and loving Him by charity, it possesses really within itself That which it knows and loves.

This contentment becomes one of startling intensity when, in certain conditions of prayer the soul passes from knowing that God dwells within it to realising His presence. This experience is one that is fraught with intense happiness. The soul not only knows that God is there present within itself, but it ' feels '[5] that

[4] Not in its *esse physicum* but in its *esse intentionale*.

[5] The word ' feels ' is of course by analogy with bodily perception. It is one that is commonly used by mystical writers to describe this ' experience ' of God indwelling in the soul.

He is present,—and present not in an attitude of majestic aloofness but in an attitude of loving tenderness towards the creature He honours with His presence. This blissful experience, though it may be accorded in a very slight and brief manner to the soul at any stage of the interior life, is had ordinarily speaking only when a good deal of progress has been made in self-abnegation, detachment and purity of soul. Normally it follows on fidelity and recollection maintained over a considerable period of time. It is something which does not, of itself, belong to the states of prayer outlined in the foregoing chapters. It carries with it a knowledge of God such as cannot be arrived at by the practice of any of the ordinary forms of mental prayer, up to and including the prayer of simplicity. As has been said it may be accorded—though in a very slight degree—at any one of the stages of development of the interior life outlined in the previous pages, especially in the final stage, but it is never the result of the soul's own efforts of intellect and will, exercising themselves in faith and charity. This ' sense ' of His presence is given by God Himself and when it occurs in a very pronounced and frequent manner it marks a definite change in the relations between the soul and God. It is a sign of definite progress beyond the ordinary ways of mental prayer.

It is a far different thing to know God (to have knowledge about Him) and to ' sense ' God—even though both kinds of knowledge be of the supernatural order and belong to the realm of faith. It is the former kind of knowledge we acquire by meditation on the mysteries of the human life of Our Lord.

By successive contemplations on that life, our outlook upon Almighty God, the world and ourselves undergoes a profound change. Each of these objects appears to us in an entirely new light, and takes up its proper position in our field of vision. This study reveals to us the meaning and purpose of our earthly existence, and the attitude we must adopt towards it in order to please God. Considering the perfection of Our Lord's life, we learn how to make our own human life a perfect one, and acquire a knowledge of the dispositions in which our existence should be fulfilled, if it is to come up to the ideal which faith and reason set before us. All this consideration is supernatural, because it is taken in view of and directed towards the attainment of our final supernatural end. It makes known to us a great deal about ourselves, our origin, our destiny, about God and His relations with us. But this knowledge does not teach us to know God with that knowledge that comes of His ' realised ' loving presence in the interior and the sense of His friendly companionship with His creature in the vicissitudes of life. The knowledge acquired in the ordinary ways of mental prayer teach us rather to know about Him. Such knowledge is little more, in itself, than a deepening of one's understanding of the ordinary truths of faith and of the mysteries of religion, an apprehending of the transformation in mind and will and conduct that conditions intimacy with God here and vision of Him hereafter, and a forming of the resolute determination to effect by the aid of grace that change in oneself which makes for close union with God. The contemplation of the Sacred Humanity is the regular means employed to achieve these objects. But if we were to think that once we had studied His Human Life, grasped the principles of His human activity, admired His virtues and lovingly tried to reproduce in our own conduct, His way of acting towards God and man—we have thereby reached the end of mental prayer, we should be mistaken. What we have done is merely to realise those human supernatural conditions in ourselves, which make union with the Divinity possible. We are meant to pass through the Sacred Humanity, to the Divinity which it veiled and clothed. All this study of the Sacred Humanity reveals God to us. It teaches us to know more and more about God in Himself and in His relations with and in His designs on us. But the knowledge we thus acquire is but feeble in comparison with that which comes when God Himself acts and by a touch makes the soul sensible of His presence. In this touch is given not only an apprehension *of the fact* of the divine presence, but also a more intimate knowing of Him Who is present. Jesus has promised this as a reward of faithful love. " He that loveth Me, shall be loved of My Father: and I will love him and *manifest myself to him.*"⁶ This manifestation of Jesus, true God and true Man, wherein the initiative is all on the side of Jesus is the normal crowning of the life of mental prayer and gives a vivid foretaste of the joys of Paradise.

When these manifestations of the glory of the Sacred Humanity become frequent and regular the soul has definitely entered on the passive stages of mental prayer. In the beginnings of this experience, the soul, in spite of the happiness it undoubtedly enjoys, suffers

⁶ St. John xiv. 21.

a great deal of anxiety. In the stage of ordinary meditation it experiences scarcely any misgivings. It is
always able to render an account to itself whether it
has well or ill acquitted itself of its exercise. The whole
process is carried on in the senses, in the imagination,
and in the understanding, and in the will (the rational
appetite that acts in conjunction with the understanding).
Everything falls within the region of ordinary consciousness and the different thoughts and affections
can be noted without any difficulty. The soul grasps
the reasons by which the will is moved to embrace
that pattern of life and action traced by Our Divine
Lord. The attraction of the will is towards the exercise
or the possession of those virtues portrayed in His
life. The soul knows about God, and about itself, all
that is necessary to direct its life according to His
desires and according to the pattern of perfection that
He has traced and enjoined. In the processes of
ordinary prayer, the intellect and the will function
according to their regular human mode ; the imagination furnishes images : the intellect abstracts ideas
from these images and the will is stirred up to love
what is presented by these ideas—in exactly the same
way as if the objects of the operations of the faculties
belonged to the natural order—to the order of things
subject to sense and to reason. Even when prayer has
attained a high degree of simplification and the work
of the understanding has become almost negligible in
comparison with the work of the will, still the
functioning of the faculties is perfectly natural. This
functioning can be apprehended and is a definite
object of consciousness.

But the revelation of God of which there is now question takes place in a mode that transcends the natural and ordinary mode of the functioning of the understanding, and is attended necessarily with a certain darkness. In this world we can never see God except through the dark veil of faith. He cannot be the idea of our intellect without faith disappearing and yielding place to vision, and this happens only in the life to come. What takes place then? God makes His presence *felt*, as it were, to the intellectual part of our soul. The intellect has no clear intellectual vision of its object but it has nevertheless a *perception* of God's presence. It is a spiritual feeling, a kind of *awareness* rather than a spiritual sight. It is impossible to see God as He is in Himself and live. God does not actualise the soul to such a vision in this world, except perhaps transiently, as some say was the case with Moses and St. Paul. Why then does He impart this vague, dark, indefinable sense of His presence? It is because the will cannot be set in motion except in consequence of an excitation of the intelligence. And at this perception of the presence of God the will is moved with an ardent impulse towards the lovable object perceived or felt to be present in the soul. The movement of love excited, is not an affection towards any created thing, e.g. virtue—act—disposition, etc., or any created representation of the Uncreated, but towards God as He is in Himself. For though we cannot in this world see God, as He is in Himself, we can love Him as He is in Himself. In this spiritual experience of which the passive character is very pronounced, the activity is nearly all of the will, and consists for the most part in a longing for union with God—and in a desire to express love of Him and to increase in that love. The action of the intellect is obscure, and is not capable of being analysed or rendered in terms of the understanding. The soul is conscious of nothing but movements of love of God in the will, whilst the faculty of thinking and reasoning, not having ideas to foster and so excite these movements, is inoperative.

According as God's direct action tends to replace the normal exercise of intellect and will, the soul in the beginning of this new state becomes haunted with the suspicion that it has become idle and inert. It believes that progress is arrested because it cannot mark any longer in itself these energetic exercises of its faculties which, for it, constituted signs of well executed mental prayer. Consequently it is plunged in uneasiness and unrest. In the way of meditation it was perfectly easy to follow the gradual change of disposition that takes place, to note the increase in knowledge of and love of Divine things, to trace the growing familiarity with the ways and mind of Jesus, and to mark the disappearance of taste for earthly things. The soul could, therefore, find perfect satisfaction and contentment in this state. But this satisfaction is denied it when meditation ceases and the higher form of affective prayer with the character of passivity takes its place. God touches the intellect and enters into and seizes the will—causing the soul to enter into a kind of activity which it can understand but vaguely, for it is to a great extent above all understanding. But still the joy is immense because at last and only in this way, by the intimate realisation of the physical presence of God in the soul, the soul experiences that its cravings after infinite happiness are beginning to be satisfied. The soul must yield itself up to the happiness of this touch of God and be content not to understand what it is going through, and it must cease from all anxious questionings as to whether it is advancing or retrograding in intimacy with its Creator. It must submit to be in darkness with regard to everything and follow with docility the advice given it by its Director regarding the way it is to comport itself during and after prayer.

When the will is thus powerfully drawn towards God, by a movement impressed on it by God Himself, it sometimes happens that the soul becomes, as it were, intoxicated with the happiness that it experiences and with the pain accompanying it. For the more it loves, the more it desires to love, and the more keenly alive it is to the amount of perfection its love lacks and which it needs to make union complete. But the pain it experiences in its anxious desires to supply what is needed to attain the utmost measure of affection, is itself a kind of happiness. The soul no longer makes use of sustained reasonings—all it does is to express in every way it can invent, its love for God, and for Him alone. It never judges it has said enough, and it never tires as long as the movement lasts. When this urge is less evident in its effects, the soul rests peacefully in God, in an attitude of self-surrender, sinking as it were into Him in silent adherence to His loving action. And in the fire of its pure love for God affection for everything out of relation to God is burned

away. Not only does it choose God before and above
all things, but in these movements every earthly thing
fades into absolute insignificance. The soul struggles
to possess the unique object of its choice more and
cannot; it yearns to make its love transform it more
into God, and its desires are baffled. And the pain it
feels at the futility of its efforts, is an act of love which
carries its charity to a higher pitch. It is intoxicated
with God, and there is scarcely a return on itself.
There are many souls that pass through this experience,
though its intensity varies much, and in some cases
the experience may be only slightly perceptible and of
short duration.

May not that which fell to the lot of Peter and James
and John on the heights of Thabor be assimilated to
the spiritual experience outlined in the preceding
pages? These three had been constantly with Our
Lord, had enjoyed His intimacy, had grown to love
His human qualities and had in their humble way
striven to imitate His ways and conform their own
way to His. It was for them the ordinary way of mental
prayer. But one day Our Lord took them apart and
led them up into a high mountain away from the
sounds and sights and attractions of earth. And there
before their eyes, He allowed the Divinity to shine
through the transparent robe of His Sacred Humanity.
The vision of His Divinity threw them into a stupor
—transcending as usual the operations of the understanding—the Scripture says, "they were struck with
fear". This was evidently not the ordinary passion of
fear which is accompanied by sadness and distress, for
the Apostles were, on the contrary, transported with

joy. Their fear was the bewilderment that the human always experiences at contact with the Divine. But this first instinctive movement past, there followed the impulse of the will to embrace, possess and hold for ever the object dimly perceived. Time disappeared, the earth faded away, their worldly ambitions vanished —and they desired nothing but to continue for ever in the enjoyment of the vision vouchsafed to them, "Let us build here", said St. Peter, "three abiding places where we can remain for ever". Consumed with love, desire, vision, intoxicated with the happiness that he felt at the first glimpse of the Divinity through the sacred veils of the Humanity, he uttered nonsense, as lovers do in the delirium of their love : the Scripture tells us, "He knew not what he said".[7] But this was not to last. God spoke from heaven saying : "This is my beloved Son : hear ye Him ";[8] explaining that life was not to be spent in the enjoyment of Thabor but in a faithful adherence to the doctrine of Jesus, walking in the obscurity of faith.

Then the vision passed, and they were contemplating 'only' the human lineaments of Jesus, they had to descend from the mountain, return to the ordinary ways of life and resume their existence ; to walk by the way of faith and self-denial. But one moment of the happiness they had enjoyed surpassed all that earthly joys extended over centuries could yield ; and that scene they had witnessed was never to be effaced from their memories and was destined to be a support to them in the rude contests they were to endure later for Christ—"for", said St. Peter, "we made known

[7] St. Luke ix. 33.　　　　[8] St. Mark ix. 6.

to you the power and presence of our Lord Jesus Christ (but), having been made eye-witnesses of His Majesty . . . when we were with Him on the Holy Mount ".[9]

So it must be with us. These transient visitations of God must be for a memory and a help to walk with courage in the way of self-denial when the light goes out and is replaced by the obscurity of faith. We must not cling to these favours; we must be very grateful when they are given us; but we must not think that all is lost when they are withdrawn. We must be content to see no one, only Jesus in His life and actions, and be satisfied with walking in His footsteps in simplicity, humility and self-denial. And though the joys of Thabor are no more, in the depth of our souls there will be profound content. For just as Jesus was as really with the Apostles in the plains below as on the mountain above, and just as this ordinary presence was to them a continual source of happiness, so too He remains with us when we tread the beaten ways, and His abiding presence brings to us that unruffled peace which is the hallmark of souls that live for God alone.

[9] 2 Pet. i. 16–17.

PART II

METHOD IN MENTAL PRAYER CONSIDERED IN ITS FUNDAMENTAL PRINCIPLES

METHOD IN MENTAL PRAYER CONSIDERED IN ITS FUNDAMENTAL PRINCIPLES

CHAPTER X

THE VISION OF FAITH PURIFIED BY MENTAL PRAYER

"The just man liveth by faith."—Gal. iii. 11.

EVERY soul walking in the way of perfection enters into what is called a state of prayer. This state is nothing else than the habitual disposition in which the soul normally finds itself. It is something that is independent of the conscious and deliberate acts of the soul's faculties. State of prayer is a term which expresses *the degree of intimacy* that the human soul enjoys ordinarily with God; the deeper the intimacy the higher the state of prayer; the less close the intimacy, the more imperfect the state. Each soul, in the measure of its progress, is in a certain supernatural condition which marks the degree and the closeness of its relationship with God. " In order to converse in the most advantageous way with God," says the Ven. Libermann, "the soul must, in beginning its meditation, strive to put itself in the state of prayer that is peculiar to it. Doing otherwise it runs the risk of gaining little profit from its spiritual exercise. In order to know the state that is proper to us, we have only to give close attention to the interior attitude the soul adopts instinctively before God in its moments of marked recollection and fervour. A great sameness will be

143

noticed in the supernatural attitude that the soul assumes on these occasions, and that is the one that should be adopted in the regular exercise of prayer. It undergoes a change as one advances in the interior life. Often it changes—in the sense that it attains a greater perfection."[1]

Intimacy with our Creator is based upon knowledge. By this is not meant the mere acquisition by our intelligence of a number of truths concerning God or Divine things. The acquisition of theological science, no matter how profound that science may be, has no power of itself to make us better acquainted with God or to put us on terms of close relationship with Him. But when the activities of the intelligence exercised on these truths is animated, directed and informed by the infused virtue of Faith, then this intellectual activity serves to make us grow in knowledge of God, and, through knowledge, in love. Our natural activity of knowing must be elevated and enlivened by the infused intellectual habit of faith[2] in order that it may help to bring us close to God. It is written in the prophets— " And they shall all be taught of God ".[3] Our knowledge of God must be supernatural knowledge if it is to promote and perfect our spirituality. The divinity stands revealed only to the divine gaze : it is only the piercing intuition of that glance that can comprehend the Godhead as it is in Itself and for what it is in Itself. It is such a vision that alone can originate a love which pours itself out on the Divine Beauty in its full reality

---

[1] Ven. Libermann : *Ecrits Spirituels*, p. 94. cf. *Letters*, Vol. I, No. 83.
[2] All apprehension and knowledge of supernatural things cannot help us to love God so much as the least act of living faith and hope made in detachment from all things. (St. John of the Cross, Spiritual Max. 24.)
[3] St. John vi. 45, Is. liv. 13.

—as opposed to any participated or reflected forms of that Beauty. It is only the vision of God as He is in Himself that can generate a personal love of God as He is in Himself. That vision and that love belongs by nature to God alone, and is for that reason called supernatural. But God in His mercy deigns to call us to share the contemplation which belongs to Himself. By infusing the divine gift of Faith into the human intellect He elevates that faculty and, giving it a participation of His own Divine Intuition, He enables it to contemplate—in a veiled manner in this world, clearly in the next when faith gives way to vision— the same Divine Beauty which He Himself eternally sees and loves.[4] It is only this vision of God, seen by the eyes of faith, that can issue in sanctity—which is nothing else than the surrender of the will to the charms of the Divine Beauty. No philosophical knowledge no matter how great, can cause the very smallest degree of this love. It is knowing God as a child knows its own parent, not knowing a great deal about God, that sanctifies the soul. The vision of God that alone can make us holy is God's Vision of Himself; it is by the love in which that vision issues that we are perfected.

The vision of God is given us in this world truly, though imperfectly, by Faith. Faith is nothing else than the supernatural, obscure intuition (not face to face) of God, which whilst always remaining obscure in the condition of this world, can nevertheless grow in intensity, in purity and in depth. Since the truths which are the object of Faith infinitely surpass human

---

[4] By this infusing the divine gift resides in the intellect but submission is not compelled.

reason, whole-souled and dutiful assent to them demands a grace-inspired act of the will; and this whole-souled and dutiful acceptance of them carries with it serious moral consequences for ourselves,[5] Hence it is evident that progress in Faith tends to perfect concomitantly the will as well as the intellect. We cannot see ourselves and God in the light that streams from the Divine Intelligence without being impelled to suit our life's activities to that condition which in this light is seen to be ours. A clear view of what the Creator is and what the creature is, when that view is given in the light of Faith, constrains the creature to act in a spirit of profound adoration and unquestioning submission to the will of God. Hence, in the last resort, growth in Faith is growth in holiness; and the measure of our faith is the measure of our perfection. This explains St. Paul's glorification of this virtue in the 11th chapter of the Hebrews—" Faith ", he says " is the evidence "—that is, the clear intuition—" of things that appear not ".[6] These things " that appear not " are the mysteries of the divine life, whether that be considered as it is in the bosom of the Blessed Trinity or in the economy of its communication to human souls through the Sacred Humanity of Jesus. God alone contemplates that mysterious life in its fullness, and adequately comprehends it: " So the things also that are of God, no man knoweth, but the spirit of God ".[7]

God's holiness is a consequence of the vision of Himself which He enjoys. His love of the Divine

[5] Cf. *Christ, the Life of the Soul.* Marmion. Part II. Ch. i.
[6] Heb. xi. 1.
[7] 1 Cor. ii. 11.

reality is infinitely perfect, being in proportion to and
determined by that vision of Himself. The measure
of that vision that He imparts to us—is the measure
also of our resemblance to Him in that infinite movement of love in which He tends toward Himself. All
Holiness consists in the love of that Infinite Good.
Supernatural holiness is nothing but the gravitation of
the will towards God—of the will as carried towards
Him by the weight of Love: "Amor meus pondus
meum ".[8] Though cut off from this vision by our
condition as creatures, we attain to it by faith. By
faith, we contemplate though dimly, obscurely and
inadequately what God contemplates. "But to us
God hath revealed them by the spirit . . . Now
we have received the spirit that is of God, that we
may know the things that are given us from God ".[9]
The spirit of which St. Paul speaks is the gift of
faith and the things that are given is the Divine Life
participated.

Since faith is a participation of supernatural or divine
knowledge, the more of mere human understanding
that is found mingled with its exercise the less perfect
it becomes. The intellect in its contemplation of the
mysteries of divine life of the Blessed Trinity in Heaven
or of the Incarnate Son of God on earth, even when
elevated by the gift of faith, is prone to vitiate its
considerations by the introduction into them of
reasonings, judgments and appreciations, which are the
fruit of its human spirit. In this sense faith must
undergo a purification and its operations must have

---

[8] St. Augustine—"My love presses me as a weight ". Confess. xiii. 9.
[9] 1 Cor. ii. 10, 12.

these corrupting elements eliminated from them if man is to know God as a friend knows his friend. Such a purification takes place in the saints. The whole process of sanctity according to the teaching of St. John of the Cross, depends on this progressive elimination of the purely human elements from the operations of the virtue of Faith.[10] In the case of Christians who take but little interest in the super-natural life the faith contains a large alloy of the natural. They see God it is true, but they see Him badly. Their spiritual vision is defective. They suffer from a super-natural myopia. They resemble persons who, because of their defective eyesight, cannot see objects clearly in distinct outline and in all their details—but only dimly, obscurely and in a confused and uncertain manner. As their understanding of God depends on their spiritual sight of Him, they know Him very imperfectly and easily hold false notions concerning Him. That is the reason why so many who are said " to have the faith " are so frequently without virtue. Their faith is very superficial ; it takes but the feeblest share in the soul's activity, which is dominated by human impulse, passions, and affections. In such souls the knowledge of God is darkened and dragged down to earth by the human considerations and views that mingle with and tarnish the purity of the knowledge of faith. As long as these conditions prevail, the soul's activity will be largely human, unsupernatural and, to a great extent, uninfluenced by grace and withdrawn from the direction of the Holy Ghost.

[10] *Ascent*, Book II.

It is lamentable that so many baptised souls are thus neglectful of the gift of Faith which they possess and allow to remain latent—almost atrophied—for want of exercise. The claims of the visible world clamour powerfully in a too successful rivalry with the claims of " things unseen " ; and yet, we know that the hidden world of the supernatural life is the world of *Reality* ; and each baptised soul bears responsibility for the development of that supernatural life within. The Divine Virtue of Faith is exercised in prayer. Thus it is that prayer is an ideal means of developing faith and an ideal preparation of the soul for the reception, and increase, of that Divine gift.

"And the Apostles said to the Lord : ' Increase our Faith '."[11] Our prayer of petition will be very perfect when it attains their earnestness and is directed towards the same thing for which they prayed with such longing and such childlike simplicity, namely, an increase of Faith. Such a prayer of petition is eminently pleasing to the Saviour. The Gospels bear eloquent testimony to the great value for the soul that He attached to the virtue of Faith. The expression of it always has the effect of stirring His admiration, moving His feelings and unlocking the treasures of His Mercy. On Him an act of real faith operates like a veritable rod of Moses, for it touches His Heart and causes waters of grace to gush forth in the soul of the believer. The predilection of Jesus for this virtue should not cause astonishment. He knows full well that a man's life takes *its* colour from the depth and sincerity of his faith. The more one penetrates into

[11] St. Luke xvii. 5.

the inner world of divine realities, veiled under the happenings of the life of the Man-God on earth, the more one experiences the transforming effect of that life and the more easily one's conduct conforms to the manner of acting of Jesus. Faith that is strong cannot be inoperative. As God's vision of Himself is the source of His life of love, so our Faith, according as it is purified from the imperfections caused by the darkened condition of our soul, will issue in activities which will bear a resemblance to the divine goodness. This will develop perfection in ourselves and render us capable of effecting good in others. The whole end of meditation considered as such, is to increase, deepen and purify our Faith.

In the previous chapters there was instituted a study of the soul in its progress through the different states or conditions of prayer; that is an examination of the phases through which the soul passes in its emancipation from what is purely human and natural, in its progress in the divine intimacy and in its assimilation to God, which is the direct fruit of that intimacy.

No soul, ordinarily speaking, is taken by God into His intimate friendship unless it freely chooses to enter into those relations of friendship, and unless it consents to adopt the means by which this friendship is initiated and cultivated.[12] The soul is aided by actual graces to make this choice, but it has the fatal power to resist grace and to disregard the divine appeal. The exercise of mental prayer is the normal way by which the soul

[12] Mental prayer as an exercise is the discipline to which the soul must submit itself in order to enter into the way of union with its God.

becomes intimate with God, shares His secrets and receives His communications and spiritual gifts.[13] The details of method in mental prayer must now be considered carefully.

[13] The exercise of mental prayer must be distinguished from the state of prayer, which is its result, i.e., that in which it normally issues and which is, as was said, the position which the soul instinctively tends to adopt in the presence of God.

CHAPTER XI

"Hearken to the voice of my prayer, O my King and my God. . . . O Lord in the morning thou shalt hear my voice. In the morning I will stand before thee." Ps. v. 3-5.

§1. Method in Mental Prayer.

THERE are several methods of prayer; the differences between them are accidental. All are substantially the same in that they take account of the constitution of our human nature in tracing the path which that nature must pursue in order to get away from itself and reach God. They all point out that the activities by which that union is, in its first stages, developed, are elicited by human faculties, in a human way, though supernaturalised. The several methods differ solely in the manner in which they direct the calling into operation of the several activities. In all forms of prayer those activities are the ones which belong to us as rational creatures, namely, the activities of the intellect, the memory and the will. The imagination, a faculty which we have in common with the animals, plays its part, for the operations of our intelligence are conditioned by it. It can be a great help as well as a great hindrance: all methods of prayer must take account of it and the Ignatian method accords it a very important rôle.

So true is it that all methods are fundamentally the same, that a person that has never studied any, will instinctively follow in his approach to God, the broad

lines that they all have in common. It is by the will
and the understanding that spirit is united with spirit;
and the operations of these faculties, in human beings,
must always take place in a human way, and be conformable to human nature: this in all of us is essentially
the same. Still, it is of great utility to have a reflective
knowledge of the processes of prayer, for frequently,
because of fatigue of mind, or want of energy in God's
service or absorption in external work or for any such
cause, our entry into converse with God will lack
spontaneity, facility, and positive direction. It is in
these circumstances—when the soul is sluggish—that
method is useful. A practical grasp of the order of the
different acts which the soul must elicit, and a consciousness of the effects which, with grace, these acts produce,
will help to overcome our natural inertia, dissipate
vagueness or idle dreaming, and set the soul in movement
towards God.

§2. Remote Preparation for Mental Prayer.

Mental Prayer is confessedly difficult; but it has no
peculiar difficulties of its own; it presents none other
than those which occur in every effort of the soul to
respond to a movement of the divine as opposed to
the movement of the natural. Its difficulties are keenly
felt, solely because in it the human is more consciously
felt in presence of, and in contact with, the divine than
is the case in the ordinary circumstances of life. In
these, it is too often true that what is seemingly supernatural and under the influence of grace, is purely

natural and therefore excites no conflict or repugnance in us. But to apply ourselves to mental prayer *we must put ourselves deliberately in the presence of God* and we must make an effort to submit our souls to the divine operations—and this costs and is something against which our natural self revolts. The great difficulty then in mental prayer is not in the exercise itself but is outside of it. Yet no matter what difficulty, what pain, is involved in the work by which the soul, gathering up its faculties, sets foot, as it were, on the path of prayer, though this effort—because of original sin—runs counter to nature and is even recognised to be but the beginning of a painful progress, it is well to remember that each effort in the feeble struggle attracts the loving gaze of God and calls forth a new influx of divine energy. Moreover it is true that even if this struggle were to last for a lifetime, such a life of effort to effect contact with the supernatural would avail more than many lives spent in the more comfortable observance of what may be termed the bare essentials of the exercise of religion.

As has been said, it is only by these three faculties, intellect, will and memory,—to which may be added the imagination—that we can effect contact with God. Such contact is impossible unless these faculties are called away from the natural objects on which they find pleasure in exercising their activities. We remember what concerns us: our thoughts turn towards what interests us and our imagination busies itself with what flatters us. The faculties relinquish their objects with extreme reluctance. It requires much self-discipline and strong effort—a discipline and an effort from which the average person shrinks—to withdraw the powers of the soul from what naturally pleases them and concentrate them on the divine which has but little attraction for them. The gait of those who are summoned away from a pleasant occupation to one which is eminently disagreeable gives a lively image of the attitude of the faculties when they are called away from what appeals to them and bidden to fix themselves on God. This calling in of the powers of the soul to attach them to God as the object on which to exercise themselves is called *recollection*, that is, a gathering together and away from something else. This effort of recollection cannot be renewed day by day unless there has been made a deliberate choice by which God is preferred to all creatures and unless the soul is schooled day by day, in spite of temptations, to adhere with determination to that choice, cost what it may to nature. It must say to itself constantly : " I must have God at all costs ". It must, using the power of free election, strive to resist the visible attractions of creatures, when inordinate, and desire to surrender to the invisible beauty of God for " God does not give Himself entirely to us until we give ourselves entirely to Him ".[1] For unless there is made this preliminary surrender on our part, the exercise of prayer tends to become a mere form, if it is not rendered utterly impossible.[2] This surrender is not beyond us ; God asks it and His grace will give the strength we need.

---

[1] St. Teresa, *Way of Perfection*, Ch. xxviii.

[2] " Let no created thing have a place in your heart, if you would have the face of God pure and clear in your soul ; yea rather empty your spirit of all created things and you will walk in the divine light." (1 St. John of the Cross, Spiritual Max. 26.)

To make this exercise successfully then, *we must elicit a strong and firm determination in our will to progress in spirituality* and to overcome all the obstacles that oppose themselves to our advancement in friendship with God. We must have the will to renounce, that is aim at renouncing all inordinate attachment to things of earth (perfect renouncement comes only by degrees), and we must will to cultivate an interest in the things of heaven. This is to dispose ourselves to acquire that " poverty of spirit " to which is promised the Kingdom of Heaven.[3] To the soul that empties itself of all inordinate desire for created satisfaction, God comes with the abundance of His Gifts ; He establishes His reign in that soul. He communicates to it a knowledge and love of Himself which begets a happiness that bears an analogy with the beatitude of the blessed in Heaven. " Blessed are the clean of heart for they shall see God," said Our Lord.[4] This resolution to steel ourselves against the attraction of the things of earth, must be accompanied by endeavours on the part of our intelligence to increase in knowledge of the mysteries of our religion. For although Faith is an infused Virtue, its exercise will be paralysed unless the faculty, namely the intellect, in which it resides, becomes more and more aptly disposed for it by activity exercised on the revelation of God. Mere intellectual grasp of religious truths is useless ; but still real deepening of faith is impossible without growth in understanding of these truths. Where the study of these truths is made with humility, with a subjection of our minds to what is beyond their power to comprehend (though not to

---

[3] St. Matt. v. 3. [4] St. Matt. v. 8.

know), with a sincere desire to gain a deeper insight into the wonderful manifestations that God has made of Himself to men—the intellect is made apt to be penetrated through and through with the Virtue of Faith. The virtue itself becomes more and more deeply rooted in it and the light of the virtue compenetrates and elevates the natural light of the intellect, imparting new energy and at the same time strengthening its natural activity.

The soul has not a natural liking or taste for the study of divine things, at least for that study which has as its object an ever nearer approach to God's understanding of things, and a reforming of conduct with a view to conforming it to the pattern traced by God made Man; therefore the acquisition of a taste for spiritual knowledge involves self-conquest. So far indeed is the study of divine things from being a congenial exercise for the human intelligence that it can safely be said that a growing interest in, and a desire for, greater knowledge of spiritual things, is a sure sign that God is calling the soul to intimate friendship with Himself. A taste for spiritual books or an anxiety to hear instructions on supernatural truths is a great grace, and one for which we should often pray.

In the firm resolve of the will to renounce satisfaction in the things of the earth and in the study by the intellect of the mysteries of faith, consists the principal *remote preparation* for meditation. It leaves the two faculties through which we come in contact with God, free to exercise those activities by which that contact is effected. " For mental prayer means the occupation of our faculties upon God, not in the way of thinking or speculating about Him, but stirring up the will to conform itself to Him and the affections to love Him."[5] It is not easy for these who live in the world to acquire that poverty of spirit, that aloofness from earthly things which is a pre-requisite for mental prayer. Hence for them the practice of it presents some difficulty.[6] Those who enter religion make that poverty of spirit the condition of their lives, and therefore remove the chief obstacle to progress in intercourse with God. This of course is not sufficient. One must not remain idle and inactive, trusting to this initial grace. It is always necessary to hear the admonition of the apostle saying that it is obligatory to " stir up the grace of God which is in us " and make it effective and fruitful.[7]

We must aim at acquiring a great purity in our affections, gradually weeding out from them all that is too natural. We are brought to a standstill in our mental prayer if we allow ourselves to be held captive by inordinate affections for creatures or by an excessive regard for ourselves, our own ease and our own satisfactions.[8] Vigorous efforts must be made to get

[5] From a treatise on Mental Prayer.

[6] Many holy people in the world however, completely overcome this difficulty and become very proficient in mental prayer.

[7] St. Teresa gives an excellent warning on this :—"O my sisters, be not too secure, nor allow yourselves to sleep. . . . You know there is no thief worse than a domestic one. Since, therefore, we *are always ourselves*, if great care be not used (as is used in important affairs), and everyone do not diligently use all her endeavours to be continually denying her will, there are many things which may deprive us of this holy liberty of the spirit which we seek after, that it may fly to its Creator, without being burthened with earth and lead ". (*Way of Perfection.* Chap. x.)

[8] A man mounting a hill while dragging a cart gives us a picture of the soul that wishes to lift itself up to God without being free from anxieties and desires (cf. *Spiritual Maxims of St. John of the Cross.* No. 52 in Critical Spanish Ed., Fr. Gerard, 1912, No. 137 in English Ed. Trans. Lewis).

control over every attachment that threatens to take possession of and master us. If we are not prepared to make these efforts, or if we are too cowardly to act against our inclinations we shall impede the action of grace and fail to make progress.[*] All our passions must be kept under restraint. To allow ourselves to act with too much eagerness in anything is to surrender ourselves to the matter in which we are interested; it is to permit it, not our own soul, to control our activities. Eagerness in thought or act implies always that something has strongly gripped us. In such cases we fall under the control of something distinct from ourselves and our activities lose their autonomy, as it were. They will not be perfectly under our domination and can therefore with difficulty proceed from a principle of faith or even of reason. Feverish activity or anxiety tends to disturb the calm and balance of our interior faculties; besides, God's grace cannot make an impression upon the soul when it is in a state of agitation. Those desirous of advancing in the ways of spirituality must school themselves to act without precipitation and to preserve a certain peaceful moderation in all things. Excitement is fatal to prayer.

The same vigilance to curb the passions must be extended to our senses, interior and exterior. The imagination of each one of us is stored with images, many of which are not of things pertaining to the supernatural world. To keep one's mind prepared for God, and keep it fixed on God when prayer has

---

[*] If we are faithful in making these efforts, we may with confidence direct our petition to the giver of all grace Whom we seek: " Look thou upon me and have mercy upon me for I am alone and poor ". (Ps. xxiv. 16.)

commenced, we must have learned to exercise a great deal of control over the imagination. It must not be allowed to govern us or carry us away with it. The habit of indulgence in reverie or day-dreaming is very harmful. We must strive to store our imagination with images between which and the truths of faith or the service of God, there may be an easy connection. A continual mortification of the spirit of curiosity is a great help towards acquiring control of the imagination. The sense of sight and that of touch must be submitted to the same discipline. To expect to be a person of prayer and to accord every satisfaction, even when these satisfactions are not positively wrong, to one's senses, is to expect the impossible.[10] On the other hand it is evident that the persistent effort to make our lives a remote preparation for prayer results in real progress on the path that leads from self to God. It demands, it is true, much that is difficult and even bitter to human nature; but God's help will be abundant and response to this demand ensures that tranquillity and that liberty of spirit, which, making the soul receptive of Divine peace and light and love facilitate the communication of the hidden mysteries of God.

§3. Immediate Preparation for Mental Prayer.

The grace that God gives to the soul which He is calling to Himself, the desire of the soul to respond,

[10] To think that God will admit to His friendship a lover of his own ease is madness. (St. Teresa.) Quoted with approval by St. Alphonsus in Prax. Conf. ix. 3. cf. Chap. xvi on Mortification for fuller treatment.

and the measures that it takes to prepare itself to be
receptive of God's communications, all these consti-
tuting the remote preparation, place the soul in a
certain condition or attitude towards God. A spiritual
want now makes itself felt and one naturally looks
for some subject which will enable the intellect, the
memory and the affections to direct themselves towards
God. The immediate preparation consists in the
selection of some subject; some scene or some thought,
which will serve to put the soul in touch with God
and with itself. Although we are not capable of
analysing the matter to ourselves in the beginning,
yet the fundamental yearning and aspiration of the
soul—that which forms the undercurrent of all its
strivings—is a reaching after God Himself. This
yearning, set up in us by faith, is spiritual and supernatural. It is not a reaching out after some external
good, like position or property; nor after physical
well-being; nor yet after intellectual development.
All these are the desires of sense and mere natural
understanding. The groping of the soul of which
there is question is governed by the dim consciousness
that the attainment of the objective at which it aims
is to be effected by some kind of radical change in
itself.[11] The soul realises though in a very obscure
manner, that it is aspiring after more perfect union
with God, and at the same time is made aware by the
instincts generated in it by sanctifying grace that such
union is impossible unless it is made in some way like
to God. It vaguely understands that to be more

[11] The soul at this stage is beginning to experience for itself the deep truth
contained in Our Lord's words: "Every one of you that doth not renounce
all he possesseth cannot be my disciple". St. Luke xiv. 33.

intimate with God it must grow in resemblance with God.[12] The soul penetrated by grace has a new life, and it is the efforts of that life to expand and to develop itself that sets the soul in motion. The whole process is nothing else than the stirring of grace reaching after its own growth.

This movement of the soul must be concerned with some object. The human spirit can develop only by the activities of will and intellect. These faculties demand objects for their exercise : their activity cannot be, as it were, self-originated or self-sustained. To think, we must think about something : to will, we must desire something. Furthermore, in the present state of existence in this world, the intellect depends on the imagination for its operations. Where there is no imaginative image, there can be no intellectual idea. Now the movement of the soul stirred up by grace, supernatural though it is, must conform to the natural modes of thought. The mind even when concerned about divine things must lean on the help of the imagination. God Himself, however, presents no hold for the imagination. Hence the soul, in its efforts to produce that activity which should develop the divine life in it, is confronted with a serious difficulty. It knows that it can grow in likeness to God only through acting in a way which bears a resemblance to God's way of acting. But how can man act as man and yet act like God ? It would seem impossible. And yet in the depths of the supernatural being that is given it by grace, the soul is aware that there is an obligation on

---

[12] The word *deification* is used to express the process by which the soul is made like to God.

it, created by grace itself, to be " perfect as its heavenly Father is perfect ".[13] How can this obligation be fulfilled? God in His Wisdom, Goodness and Power has solved the difficulty.

If God were to live like man and were to do and suffer as man acts and suffers, and if He were to do all that as it becomes God to do it, then man would have had traced out for him a pattern of divine action set forth in human and therefore imitable terms. God came and acted as man, doing that with a divine perfection so that man might learn to act as God, and thus grow in likeness to God. More intimate union with God follows and is in proportion to the likeness to God. The soul is created for and destined for this union. In the life of His Divine Son on earth God showed man the path that he is to follow in order to enter into union with the Divinity. Hence He said, " this is my beloved Son—hear ye him ".[14] That is to say that we have only to contemplate and to try to reproduce in ourselves the soul-operations of Jesus Christ, in order to cause the Divine Life planted in us by Baptism to expand and reach its development. The life, the virtues, the words, the actions and the principles of Jesus form the exemplar on which our imagination can lay hold, and from which it will furnish the matter for the intellect and the will to work upon. Jesus traces the pattern of our activity. In Him that activity is the expression of the Divinity, of which He has the plenitude ; its reproduction by us is the means by which is developed in us that Divine Life of which our souls are almost empty in the beginning (for by Baptism, the soul receives as it

[13] St. Matt. v. 48.   [14] St. Matt. xvii. 5.

were, merely the germ of that life). The constant and sustained effort to copy in ourselves the life of Jesus Christ as gradually unfolded during the thirty-three years and as culminating in the passion, will work out in our persons first the purification of the senses, and then the purification of the spirit; it is only after these purifications that God can take complete possession of our souls. The imitation of the virtues of Our Lord's life necessitating as it does, fidelity to the inspirations of grace and contradiction of the movements of self, purifies the soul of inordinate desires and affections. An entry into, and a participation in, the sufferings and passion of Our Lord achieve that final purification in which the last vestiges of egoism are burned away and the soul is made ready for yet closer union with God.

The purifications are considered here actively— that is as taking place through the soul's co-operation with the Divine action. In the higher states of prayer, even in the obscure beginnings, the purifications are passive and are effected by the direct action of God.

The subject then of meditation will be taken from something connected with the life of Our Lord. One will naturally select what suits one's spiritual condition, and the manner in which the subject will be utilised will be dictated by the spiritual needs of the soul at the moment. The same subject may be taken at different stages of the soul's progress, but the mode in which it is handled will vary with the varying moods of the spiritual life. An incident in the life of Our Lord will suggest different reflections and different affections to one who is beginning and to one who has already made progress. This subject should always be prepared over night out of the Gospel itself or out of some spiritual book. One or two thoughts should be retained in the mind as those which should furnish the matter of conversation with God in the morning. A real desire for progress, if it exists, carries with it a consciousness of the obstacles to that progress existing in ourselves and a keen anxiety to obtain the grace necessary to overcome them or sweep them away. The sight of the obstacles to grace will naturally create regret for our perversity, a dislike of it and a turning to God for help to correct it. These emotions are examples of the affections which should accompany the reflections and to which the reflections should lead. Hence with the preparation of the considerations there should be determined at least in a general way the affections to which they should give rise, considering the needs of our souls.

This preparation of the subject should take place, if possible, after the contact with men and affairs necessary during the day has ceased. One should endeavour to allow no distracting thought or occupation to intervene before the morning's meditation; for such would banish from the memory the spiritual thoughts and affections that have been prepared. We should, with all possible tranquillity of spirit, and without any violent efforts of memory, strive to keep the subject of next day's prayer uppermost in our minds when retiring. If the reflections and affections are present to us when we prepare to go asleep, they will easily be recalled in the morning. Whilst dressing, our thoughts should be directed towards the Church, and should be coloured with a certain pleasurable anticipation of some spiritual advantage to be derived from the audience with Our Lord which is to take place. Each morning's exercise of meditation is an important event in our lives, for if done with good-will and with a serious effort, it will always mark an advance in intimacy with Our Divine Lord. Every fresh conversation we have with a person in whom we are interested, whom we like and whose acquaintance we are cultivating, makes us grow in intimacy with, and in knowledge of, that person. The same effect is produced by our conversations with Our Lord in prayer. Every morning's meeting with Him should be looked forward to by us as something new, fresh, and interesting in our lives, as something fraught with great possibilities for us.

This immediate preparation of meditation should never be omitted. It is not respectful to the Lord to enter into His presence to speak to Him in our morning meditation without having settled in our mind what matters we should treat of with Him. We never enter the room of a person occupying any position without our being fully prepared with the observations we intend to make, the propositions to put forward and the matters to discuss. If we were to enter, and then, when in the person's presence being asked what was the object of our visit, we were to say that we were not quite sure but that we would then and there begin to look for some subject of conversation, our reception would be rather cold and we should be politely shown to the door—our procedure would be unmannerly in the extreme. To enter a meditation without having mind and will ready for the interview with the Lord is to be guilty of very bad manners in His regard. And yet there are many souls who, quite polite in human intercourse, are frequently guilty of this grave discourtesy to the Saviour, the King of Kings, and the Lord of this world and the world to come. His forbearance with us and His magnanimity should not encourage us to treat Him with a rude and inconsiderate familiarity.

Meditation is a work of memory, intellect and will. That it be not waste of time and a tempting of God, the memory should be stored with some knowledge suited to our spiritual condition, our intellect should be prepared to consider it, and our will stirred up to adopt the resolutions that such considerations might suggest.[15]

§4. Entry into mental prayer.

From *the moment that we rise* from sleep our minds should be directed towards the audience with Our Lord that is presently to take place ; and we should come to the Church with a vivid realisation of the fact that we are really coming into the very presence of One Who means everything to us—One Who is ready

[15] To the soul who has joyfully observed all that is required as preparation for mental prayer, the words of the Psalmist are beautifully applicable : " Blessed is the man who hath not walked in the counsel of the ungodly . . . but his will is in the law of the Lord and on His law he shall meditate day and night. . . . And he shall be like a tree which is planted near the running waters, which shall bring forth its fruit in due season ". (Ps. 1.)

and willing to listen to us as we plead the interests
of our souls with Him, and finally Who has the power
to raise us to that state in which our souls will be fitted
to share His intimacy. It is a great consolation for
us to realise that He is more interested in our progress
than we are ourselves, and that in Him we shall have a
patient and tender listener Who will follow with sympathy every movement, every thought, every aspiration
of our souls during the time we spend in His presence.[16]
This reflection will enable us to enter the Church with
the same pleasurable anticipation as we have when
we enter a room where there is one awaiting us, who
is great and kind, who has the power to do immense
good, who is ever ready to help those who are in need,
and who loves us very tenderly. The consciousness of
our unworthiness should not be allowed to interfere
with this glad eagerness that we should rightly
experience at the prospect of being privileged to enjoy,
undisturbed, the society of Our Lord for half-an-hour
or more. If we will it, that is if we are willing to do our
part of what is necessary in order to have this tranquil
intercourse with Jesus, we can remain with our souls
bathed in, and enveloped by, the influence of His
presence during the whole time allotted to meditation.
All that is required of us is that, like Mary, our
thoughts, the eyes of our spirit as it were, should be
fixed on Him the whole time.

This involves *recollection*, that is, the gathering up
of the activities of our memory, our understanding
and our will to prevent them from being exercised on

[16] " If a soul is seeking after God, the Beloved is seeking it much more,"
St. John of the Cross. *The Living Flame of Love*, Stan. iii. 30.

any other object than on one connected with His life, His actions, His virtues, His thoughts, His sufferings.[17] This dwelling on the mysteries of Our Lord's life may —in fact, should—be accompanied by a certain return on ourselves; His feelings, emotions, acts, experiences should be contrasted with ours. This contrast between the perfection manifested in Him and the perversity revealed in us, generates detestation of the perversity and the desire to become more conformed to the Saviour.[18]

The sight of the tabernacle with the lamp burning before it, as we enter the Church (i.e., if the meditation be made in Church), reminds us that therein resides the Great God of Heaven and Earth, the Sovereign Lord and Saviour of mankind, Who, clothed in the flesh, lived that scene on earth or exercised that virtue which we have selected to review in His presence, and about which we intend to converse with Him, with regard to its bearing on our own inner life. The thought of His infinite perfections and the plenitude of the Divinity which resides in Him in its fulness should cause us instinctively to fall on our knees before Him, in an attitude of profound adoration and reverence. This exterior act of worship should be the outward expression of our interior submission—the prostration of our whole being before the Majesty of God made man involves the homage of our understanding, of our will and of all our faculties of body and soul. It will help if, with eyes closed, we imagine Him in front of us, while we keep ourselves in this humble position

[17] The difficulty of recollection has been treated on p. 155.
[18] This point will be developed later on when treating of the body of prayer.

before Him. But the act itself must be one of the will really directing all the powers to take up this attitude that becomes the creature in the presence of the Creator. This inner act of worship should reflect and express itself externally in a devout and respectful position of the body. The effort to assume and maintain this posture of deep respect will react upon the interior, and give ease, force and vividness to the inner dispositions of mind and heart. *The initial act of adoration* is of great importance; it will repay the effort to make it with full consciousness and actuality of intention, for, if well made, it is in itself sufficient, oftentimes, to secure the success of our meditation.

The presence of God to us that is a consequence of these acts of the intelligence and the will deliberately directed towards Him, is a profound reality. God is present also to the slothful, the heedless, the distracted and the indifferent, but in a totally different manner. He is present to such persons as one is present to those to whom one is near but by whom one is not observed. But to the devout worshipper He is present as the kind benefactor is to the person on whom a kindness is lovingly bestowed.

It is only by faith that we can conceive of God as present in this way. Reason by itself could only reveal to us God as present in us and all around us as the First Cause of all things. This is the omnipresence known to philosophy. Our first act of *Adoration* then implies an act of Supernatural *Faith*. " We adore that which we know."[19] This act of Faith may regard its object

[19] St. John iv. 22.

in various ways—all good, but not all equally effective.
Some will, by an effort of the imagination, represent
God to themselves as seated before them on a throne
of majesty and themselves prostrate in worship at His
feet. Others will prefer to fix their thoughts on the fact,
without any pictorial representation, that God is
present in the Tabernacle before them. St. Teresa
loved to think of God as dwelling in the depths of her
soul and of herself as pouring out all her desires and
longings and emotions at His feet.[20] The more ordinary
manner, especially in the beginning, is to worship God,
in Jesus Christ, presented before us by imagination,
in the mystery which has been chosen as the subject
of prayer. However the initial act of worship be made,
the faculties must be brought back to be occupied about
the mystery as if it were taking place at the actual moment
of the meditation. One must, as it were, annihilate
space and time and transporting oneself in spirit to
the actual epoch at which our Lord walked on earth,
live over with Him again the event that is being contemplated, and strive to excite in the heart the feelings
that would have been stirred were one present with
Him in these circumstances. If one has given way to
distractions the return to our Lord is comparatively
easy when the imagination has been strongly impressed
by the details of the mystery. When a good deal of
progress has been made in the interior life, when the
spirit by frequent contemplations has been steeped in
the inner dispositions of the Sacred Humanity, and when
the imagination, grown sluggish, no longer lends itself
easily to the "composition" of details, the soul can

[20] cf. St. Fr. de Sales : *Devout Life,* ii. c.2.

adopt another simpler and more direct way of putting itself in the presence of the Lord.

The soul can represent to itself the Divine Master living in the depths of its own interior—as He really is in His Godhead[21] ; it can consider Him there as the source of the Divine Life which it possesses in some little measure and can regard itself seated at His Feet in the position of Mary, developing its considerations as if He were giving ear to them, and holding itself attentive to receive the impulses of the graces that are internally flowing from His Sacred Heart : " Virtue went out from Him and He healed all ".[22] The exercise of prayer can be made in this way even when there is a formal contemplation of an actual scene from the life of Jesus. The soul can represent to itself the whole series of events,—the sayings, the actions and the rest— that the mystery comprises, as taking place in the midst of itself, with Jesus as the centre. It is to be remembered that spirit is present to spirit solely by the operation of its two spiritual faculties, and chiefly by the operation of the will. We can therefore maintain ourselves under the sanctifying influence of the proximity of Jesus, as long as we keep our thoughts and affections fixed on Him. This means an effort on our part to withdraw our thoughts, our imaginations and our interests from everything that is not Himself. Furthermore, when, through distraction or through some other cause, we have withdrawn ourselves from His divine influence

---

[21] St. Teresa describing her prayer in its early stages says : " I contrived to picture Christ within me, and I used to find myself the better for thinking of those mysteries of His life in which He was most lonely ". *Autobiography* ix. The whole passage should be read.

[22] St. Luke vi. 19.

we have the power to place ourselves under it once more, by an act of the will, recalling our wandering faculties.

The deep sense of the nearness of God bringing, as it does, some taste of that peace which the world cannot give should inspire us with a deep feeling of *gratitude* for the happiness of being admitted into His Presence : for in the light of His Holiness and Goodness we cannot fail to recognise how unworthy we are to appear before Him owing to our own misery, worthlessness and incapacity for all good. His perfect purity and justice reveals in a strong light—proportioned to our faith—our own sinfulness. We realise that apart from the grace of God we are nothing and can do nothing, and that of ourselves we are utterly devoid of virtue. The light of God's presence shows us that if there is any virtue in our souls, it is entirely due to Him, and that we have nothing of ourselves except resistance to His grace and the nullifying of His favours. Thus the acts of Faith and Adoration logically issue in one of profound *Humility*. But this expression of abasement must be filial, not servile ; it must be more akin to reverence than to shrinking fear, and must be accompanied by a peaceful *confidence* that the Lord, who has shown Himself in so many ways good to His creature, will pity the imperfections of that creature, enable it to overcome its vicious inclinations and help it to advance in the way of holiness. We know that God cannot love except Himself ; He can love *us* then, only in so far as He finds Himself in us. We have experienced His love and we expect with confidence that He will impart to our souls that which will enable Him to love those souls ever more and more—by imparting to them an ever increasing participation in His own life.

The consideration of God's goodness, of our own great needs, and of the ardent desires that we feel in ourselves to have these needs supplied, inspires us with the hope of obtaining our request. From the depths of our hearts we send up a strong *supplication* to the Holy Ghost that He would impart light to our intelligence and strength to our memory, that we may be able to penetrate deep into the meaning of the mystery on which we are about to meditate. We should beg, in addition, that He would impart strength and vigour to our will that we may be able to give effect to the good desires aroused in us by our deeper understanding of the subject of meditation. Finally, we should ask that the Holy Spirit would so direct and guide us that all the acts and movements of the soul elicited during the ensuing prayer should be for the glory of God and for our own spiritual progress.[23] These acts of the presence of God, of Faith, Adoration, Gratitude, Humility, Confidence and Supplication for Light and Strength, constitute the Introduction or entrance into the body of prayer which is made up of considerations and affections. If the soul, in making these preliminary acts, which as a rule need not occupy much time, finds a particular savour in any one of them, it need not force

---

[23] These preliminary remarks find beautiful expression in the inspired words :—" Hear O Lord my prayer ! enter not into judgment with Thy servant for in Thy sight no living man shall be justified . . . turn not away Thy face from me . . . make Thy way known to me wherein I should walk, for I have lifted up my soul to Thee . . . teach me to do Thy Will, for Thou art my God . . . Thy good spirit shall lead me into the right land. . . . For Thy name's sake, O Lord, Thou wilt quicken me in Thy Justice ". (Ps. cxlii.)

itself to pass on. If, for instance, it finds a great satisfaction in its act of adoration and feels a desire to remain in the interior attitude of deep worship before its Creator, it may continue to abide in that disposition of worship. It can so remain until the impulse to go on to the other preliminary acts or to the body of the meditation, comes to it.

CHAPTER XII

THE BODY OF MENTAL PRAYER

*"This is my beloved Son, in whom I am well pleased :
hear ye him."* St. Matt. xvii. 5.

ALL sanctity is effected in us by contact with
the Sacred Humanity ; this contact is created
by our willing contemplation of the great
mystery of the Incarnation. We posit the condition of
our advancement in the interior life by living with Jesus
during His earthly pilgrimage, listening to His instructions, accompanying Him in His journeys, studying His
actions, admiring His virtues and assisting at His sufferings. The nature and number of the considerations to
which the exercise will give rise, will correspond to our
spiritual condition, that is, to the degree in which the life
of Our Lord has been applied to ourselves and is being
lived by us. Every thought which we elicit must be
directed to the moving of our will to adhere to God, to
accept His will, and to embrace the means of fulfilling it,
and to accept the happenings of life in the spirit of Jesus.

§1. The Exercise of Prayer for Beginners.

In the beginning when the soul is just emerging from
the life of nature, the work of the intelligence is to form
strong convictions on the fundamental truths of religion.
Its work is to create not a mere speculative belief in
the necessity of living one's life on earth as a preparation
for the next world, but a practical conviction of the

absolute necessity of saving one's soul and of adopting the best means to secure that end. The things of heaven are weighed in the balance against the things of earth and are elected as being of infinitely greater value. The attraction which the world exercises is recognised to be an obstacle to salvation; therefore that attraction must be combated vigorously. The principles which pass current in the world are seen to be opposed to those of God and it is incumbent on us to destroy their hold on our minds. We face the fact that if we are to secure heaven we must learn to regard things differently from the way in which they are viewed by worldlings— and from the way in which we considered them ourselves a short while since. Our standards of value are to be changed. In one word, we labour to form in ourselves a deep and practical conviction of the truth of Our Lord's words, " What doth it profit a man if he gain the whole world and suffer the loss of his own soul ? "[1] Sin must be eliminated and the passions that tend to drag us into offences against God must be kept in check.

At first our convictions are weak and ineffectual; passions and faults darken our mind and do not allow these supernatural truths to get hold of and penetrate our soul. Creatures occupy and absorb our affections. Divine things make little appeal to us. The will is difficult to move and countless attractions tie it down to earth. A great deal of reflection, comparison, consideration and petition for Divine help is necessary for us in order that the new ideas, the new standards, the new outlook should be thoroughly grasped and should issue in practical determination to reform our

[1] St. Matt. xvi. 26.

life. The whole function of meditation at this stage is to create " idées forces ",[2] in the supernatural order. The sense of our past disorders, our present weakness, and the possibility of future failure is present with us during all these considerations and it moves us to make strong appeals to Our Lord for His light, help, and encouragement. These are what are called the affections which it is the object of the considerations to produce. They are meant to intermingle with the reflections.

At this period most of the time of prayer is given to reflection—and affections are elicited with difficulty.[3]

But when the intelligence under the influence of grace has perseveringly laboured to form in itself Divine Truth, and when the will has repeatedly and even violently forced itself to withdraw from adherence to creatures, and to move towards God, gradually a change takes place—the labour of the intellect becomes less, the need of force (on the part of the will) diminishes little by little. Thus by the operation of Divine Grace, and in accordance with the law of habit, a change is effected which is a progress. The soul now experiences the truth of the inspired words, " Draw nigh to God : and He will draw nigh to thee ".[4] Now the time required for consideration is not so great a part of the whole, and the will more easily turns to God—affections

[2] Meaning " ideas calculated to induce action ".

[3] St. Teresa's words contain useful advice :—"These souls are almost always occupied with the work of the understanding, in discourse of meditation, and they do well, because more is not given to them. Still, it would be good sometimes, to employ themselves in making acts of love and praise of God, doing it as best they can, for these acts powerfully excite the will ". (Interior Castle. 4th Mansions. Chap. i. 7.)

[4] St. James iv. 8.

are elicited with less difficulty. This change continues until, by degrees, the soul passes into the more advanced stage which we have now to consider.

§2. The Exercise of Prayer for Those More Advanced.

When the soul has succeeded in definitely breaking with the domination of the passions, and formed the conviction that it must at all costs serve God and preserve itself in sanctifying grace by His aid, then its activities in prayer take a new direction. As this is the condition of most souls that are aiming at leading a spiritual life, it will be necessary to develop at more length the manner of prayer which is adapted to this stage.

It is no longer the warnings of Jesus with regard to the dangers of the world, the difficulties of salvation and the dreadful fate that awaits those who misuse the chances offered them, that constitute the theme on which the understanding exercises itself; the soul dwells, preferably, on His Personality and on the virtues through which that personality manifests itself. Jesus is no longer listened to as a teacher of morals, but rather studied as a model of perfection. The soul realises that being as yet but poorly established in virtue it is exposed at each instant to lapse into sin or imperfection. It knows that unless it has acquired those fixed and settled dispositions in mind and will by which it can with some facility elicit right acts, it can have no stability in the way of holiness or abide in the friendship of God. Until habits of virtue are formed, sustained virtuous action for any length of time is morally impossible. The soul sighs after that condition in which it can be strong to resist the assaults of Satan, and in which it can serve God with facility, without having before it the dread prospect of being dragged back into sin and severed by its own frailty from the society of God. It realises with keen anxiety that as long as it is under the influence of bad habits and not possessed of good ones, it has but a precarious hold on the spiritual life. There is no effort of thought required to be convinced of this. The soul having once tasted the peace and happiness that accompanies the feeling of being at peace with God and the object of His love, is all eagerness not to forfeit that peace and happiness. Yet, at each moment of the day it is being called upon to act. Life must be lived, the hourly task demands speech, or judgment or action ; and the first clash of contact with practical life reveals to the poor soul—now supernaturally sensitive—the futility and imperfection of much of its activity. That activity is seen to be, not such as will bind it closer to God, but such rather as will separate it from Him, because, for the most part, it has no claim on His approval. The soul feels keenly that its thoughts, actions and judgments in a multitude of cases are utterly unlike what Jesus would say or do if placed in similar circumstances. And it knows as well that it can please God and be united with Him in the exact degree in which it resembles Jesus in dispositions, judgments and conduct. In order to keep close by God the soul is anxious to do what is pleasing to Him, but in spite of its best efforts it fails. It knows that it must be so until it has acquired the Christian virtues, and it is filled with an ardent longing to be possessed of them.

Instinctively it turns to the study of the life of Jesus Christ on earth, in order to penetrate itself with an understanding of the manner of acting or suffering of Our Divine Lord. It is not content to view the mystery in its external aspect as it strikes the senses; it aims at piercing through this to the interior movements, emotions, feelings and thoughts of the Man-God. It strives to trace back the word or the action to the virtue in which it has its source; and labours to form to itself an idea of that human character which thoroughly pleased—satisfied, if the expression be permitted, Almighty God.[5] The Gospel lays before us a picture of a perfect human life which, whilst remaining human, is all divine. Its pages present us with a picture of virtue in act. We see portrayed, Adoration, Prayer, Service of God, Zeal for His Service, Reverence in His Presence, Love of Souls, Devotedness, Disinterested Charity, Prudence, Temperance, Benignity, Kindliness, Simplicity, Condescension, Humility, Obedience and Fortitude carried to the utmost limit. In Our Lord's soul was every human virtue compatible with His state, and every incident of His earthly existence calls one or more of them into activity. Meditation consists in dwelling upon those incidents, studying their details and from those rising to an understanding of the perfect dispositions of Heart and Soul of Him Who is the centre of each scene. We consider how perfectly Our Lord acted in each case, and then under the influence of His grace we are led to turn back upon ourselves and contrast with His our manner of acting; for instance, a consideration of His patience reveals our own

[5] " This is my beloved Son in whom I am well pleased. " (St. Matt. iii. 17.)

impatience; we set His forbearance over against our intolerance; His humility against our pride; His fortitude against our weakness; His firmness in good against our repinings and even rebellion, and so on. This or some such return upon ourselves is necessary if meditation on the life of Our Lord is to produce abundant Fruit.[6]

Dwelling by thought on Our Lord in the actions of His Life, and grasping by our faith the truth that those thirty-three years were one long act of love for us, it is impossible that we should not be moved to love one who is so lovable, or at least to desire that we should have some love to give in return to one who has been and is so devoted to us.[7] The charm of the personality of Jesus wins us to the admiration of the virtues which that personality exhibited and to long to possess those virtues. The ideal set before us by Our Divine Lord stands clear and radiant and against its radiance is seen the dark picture of our vileness and continued infidelities. This fills us with shame and confusion. An acknowledgment of our unworthiness, of our want of virtue, and an act of profound humility in which we prostrate that unworthiness before the Infinite Purity, Justice and Goodness of Our Divine Lord, spontaneously rise from the soul when confronted

[6] It must always be remembered, however, that return upon ourselves is not the essential activity and such return must be interwoven with abundant petition for Divine Light. Any concentration on self not directed and controlled by a supernatural impulse and movement of grace is likely to beget mere natural activity if not to degenerate into morbid self-analysis.

[7] The soul need never fear to spend much time in such movements towards love. They are supremely efficacious in the process of sanctification. Since Our Lord is " the Way " not only because He exemplifies and merits holiness for us, but also, because He communicates it, the soul's response to these impulses of love (a response which for the most part consists in a ' yearning ' and a ' listening ') will carry it far and quickly on the path of prayer towards union with God.

with the contrast which our dispositions and way of acting present to His. And not only do we realise in the light poured on us from the Holiness of the Heart of Jesus, that we are destitute of all goodness, but also there comes to us the harassing thought that this absence of virtue is due to ourselves, due to our resistance to grace, and to our multiplied sins and infidelities in the past. This reflection will cause the sincere soul to be penetrated through and through with compunction.

This return upon ourselves will be still more effective if we particularise it, that is, if we contrast Our Lord's way of acting with ours in similar circumstances of daily occurrence, or when brought in contact with certain persons with whom we are often associated. Our self-seeking and our want of Charity will stand out with great distinctness and will appear detestable when we have established loving, sympathetic contact with the selflessness and charity of Jesus as revealed in some incident of His life. There easily follows a resolution to be more Christ-like on these particular occasions (in which we have formerly failed), to deal more charitably with those persons, to be more considerate and less selfish.[8] As it is always more profitable to consider our want of virtue not merely

---

[8] In these returns on ourselves it is on the clear light of Jesus rather than on the activity of our own intellect that we must rely for the true vision of what we are. Intellect may and should be exercised in reflections on the actions, emotions, etc., of Our Lord, but having thus drawn near, we seek the vision of self especially as He reveals it in the light of His love. " He that followeth Me, walketh not in darkness ". (St. John viii. 12.) Having done our part we may rely on Him to give the necessary light. It usually comes in flashes without much activity on our part. Drawing near to Our Lord in sincerity—by an earnest prayerful study of Him—we become conscious of our vileness ; as a child is aware of its limitations in the presence of "grown ups ", as a savage realises his inferiority in the presence of the civilised man.

in the abstract, but also as exhibited in certain concrete cases, so, too, our *resolutions* should be of two kinds : first, a general one, to strive to imitate Our Divine Lord in His ways of life—to constitute Him our way—and then, in the second place, to determine to reproduce the features of His conduct in some selected circumstance of our life, where we signally fail. Having had so frequently experienced the ill success of our efforts in the way of virtue, we are deeply conscious of our inability to give effect of ourselves to our resolutions and we turn in confidence and humility to our Lord to *beseech Him* to give us in abundance the graces that He has merited for us in order that we may be able to conform ourselves to Him, as His heavenly Father has enjoined on us. We can plead that injunction as a reason why our prayer should be granted. The Father has asked us to walk in the footsteps of Jesus : we must obey His word : we have tried and have not succeeded ; it is incumbent on the mercy and compassion of Him Who became Man for our sakes to help us to fulfil that divine command. And then, if we have been called to stand in special relations to Jesus, as priests or as religious, there is another and stronger reason why He should not refuse us His graces, in order that we may be more worthy of the exalted position we occupy with regard to Him. And if we have been called to guide, to instruct and to be an exemplar for others, holiness is still more incumbent upon us, and our position makes a still stronger appeal to the mercy of the Lord for His efficacious grace. In this way, reflections on our various needs will suggest reasons which we may urge with God in order to persuade Him to hear us.

Our *demands* should be made with fervour, with confidence and with a strong insistance combined with reverence. We may use a certain boldness though we should not allow any undue familiarity to appear in our relations with our Creator. We may be bold because even if He is our Creator He is also our Father, and is ready to give all good gifts to His children. We shall please Him best by not being niggardly in our demands : we must dare to ask a great holiness, a great purity of heart, and a high degree of prayer and union. We shall be heard in proportion to the ardour of our desires. In all these affective acts we may address ourselves directly to Jesus, Who is God as well as Man, or we may direct our petitions to God the Father, asking Him to grant them through the merits of His Divine Son made Man. The prayers of the Church take this latter form.

In conclusion we should *invoke* the advocacy of the Blessed Virgin and that of those Saints towards whom we may have a devotion. It is a useful thing to combine our prayer with the liturgy ; hence our desires should be in harmony with the spirit of the liturgical season as expressed in the prayers of the Mass and in The Divine Offices : in union with the Church we should implore the help of the saint of the day, in order to obtain through his intercession the grace to be able to practise those virtues which he exhibited in his life.

Such is ordinary prayer in its main outlines—with its introduction, its conclusion and its principal theme. The Body of the Prayer consists of Consideration, Admiration, Contrast, Self-Abasement, Regret, Desire, Resolution and Petition. This is the logical order of the acts, and in mental prayer that is successful, all of them will usually be made, at least implicitly. But this is not necessary : if the soul feels attracted to abide in any one single affection without feeling an inclination to pass on to another it is better for it to follow its attraction and pass the whole time in the exercise of that particular affection. Those acts of the will should not be allotted a time distinct from that given to the considerations; there should be no rigid line of demarcation between the two : the considerations should always merge naturally into the affections.

The reflections are to be made as if we were studying the subject and giving expression to the thoughts to which it gives rise in us, in the presence of a sympathetic listener, who is ready to aid us by the illumination and strengthening of His grace. This Divine Listener, as has been said, may be regarded as dwelling in the interior of our being, or may be considered outside of or in front of ourselves, if that way is more helpful. To receive this aid from Him it is well to make certain pauses or complete cessations in the activities of will and understanding (as far as that is possible) and to hold the soul in an attitude of attention to the inspiration of the Divine Spirit. The Divine Spirit operates powerfully during those moments of silence and recollection, though such action remains, in normal conditions, imperceptible to us.[9]

[9] In this connection Fr. Lallemont's words are of interest :—"It is an error in prayer to constrain ourselves to give it always a practical bearing. We excite and disquiet ourselves in resolving how we shall behave on such and such occasions, what acts of humility, for example, we shall practise. This way of meditating by consideration of virtues is wearisome to the mind, and may even possibly produce disgust. Not but that it is well to do this when we pray, to foresee occasions and prepare ourselves for them ; *but it should be done with freedom of mind,* without refusing to yield ourselves to the simple recollection of contemplation when we feel ourselves drawn

In our consideration we should not be content with one view of the subject, but should turn it over and consider it under its various aspects ; first, we should study it in itself, in order that it may lay secure hold on the imagination. If this faculty is gripped forcibly by the theme we shall have a strong help against distractions, and shall experience little difficulty in recalling our faculties whenever they stray from God. In the second place, we must study the subject in relation to ourselves, in relation to the supernatural qualities we need to develop, the defects that we wish to overcome, and the vices that we desire to extirpate. But the end of prayer being not the mere acquisition of virtues, but union with God, and union with God being the effect of charity, it is the acts of the will, in which faculty charity resides, that are of primary importance ; the operations of the intellect are subordinated to them and are of value in so far as they call forth these acts of the will. These are the affections. The word should not mislead us into thinking that these should manifest themselves in an emotional way. The will is spiritual and its activity need not necessarily cause any feelings. It is quite possible to produce a strong affection and remain entirely unmoved as far as our sensitive nature is concerned.

§3.   Application and Example.

At the commencement of our prayer we are to represent to ourselves Our Divine Lord as He was in

---

to it. For then Our Lord in the course of one single meditation will endow a soul with some particular virtue and even with many virtues in a far higher degree than would be acquired in several years by these external acts ". *Sp. Doctrine*, Prin. ii. Sec. ii. ch. iv.

the mystery which we are contemplating, retracing in our memory and in imagination some of the circumstances which were the setting of that mystery. It is not necessary, and could be harmful, to retrace those circumstances in too much detail; they might divert us from the main consideration; for the regard of our soul should be fixed on the person of Our Divine Lord Himself. With the eye of Faith we must picture Him, to ourselves, according to the dispositions in which He was at the time as revealed to us by His own words on the occasion, or by the words of the Evangelist. His interior attitude thus reproduced in our imagination aids us to pass beyond the veil of external historical circumstances and penetrate into the secrets of His soul. By grace and faith we can discern what passes there. This effort to read the Heart of Jesus should be made with the same eager sympathy with which we strive to interpret the thoughts and feelings of those whom we love, when we are in their company, and perceive that they are labouring under some strong emotion. What our love reveals to us will excite us to adoration, respect, compassion, thanksgiving, etc., according to the subject. These acts will spring naturally from our souls if we realise vividly to ourselves the presence of Our Lord.

This proximity to Him is not a fiction of the imagination; it is a reality. We can converse with Him, address our thoughts and aspirations towards Him, express sympathy with Him, as we should have done were we near Him when He was on earth. This can be made clear by a concrete example. Let us, for instance, represent Our Lord as He was presented by Pilate to the people. The imagination easily pictures the immense crowd that thronged the space before the Pretorium; it can conjure up the cruel expression on those faces upturned to see the Saviour led forth by the soldiers from Pilate's hall, and the horrid execrations that burst from their lips, as He appeared. One can see Jesus crowned with thorns, covered with wounds, streaming with blood, and clothed in the miserable mockery of a royal mantle. His head is bent slightly forward, and His Divine eyes range with pity over that hostile crowd. In spite of the cruel extremity to which He is reduced, His presence dominates the scene; a tranquil majesty, rising superior to outrage and insult, radiates from His figure. In His Heart is the resolve to endure all for the salvation of men, even for those howling for His blood, and to carry out to its last exigency the will of that Heavenly Father to Whose service He had devoted every moment of His mortal life. No anger against His undeserved fate, no hatred of those who hated Him to death, only compassion for their waywardness, found place in His magnanimous Heart. His love for them triumphed over the worst efforts of their hostility. One instinctively prostrates oneself before a person who is so high-souled. After the act of adoration the soul asks itself why our Lord, though worthy only of glory, praise and honour, accepted to undergo such humiliations. He who is the source of all gladness is plunged in desolation; the All-powerful Who could, with a simple act of the will, destroy His persecutors, stands there with His hands bound and at the mercy of His creatures. Why all that? To expiate sin, and our sins amongst the number. What gratitude do we not owe for such disinterested love, and what horror should we not have for that evil which has caused such suffering! The soul should be penetrated through and through with a hatred of sin, and bitter sorrow for ever having committed it. Humility, Contrition, Love, are the fruit of those reflections. Furthermore, He Who was innocent endured all this unjust treatment without a murmur, and we rebel against all harsh treatment, even when we deserve it. And in fact we who have sinned can never be dealt with unjustly by creatures, since we are real criminals.

In this way should our considerations be intermingled with affections—each thought should suggest an appropriate act of the will. The whole exercise should thus end in an ardent longing to reflect in our own conduct what we have seen in Our Divine Model, and in a disposition to remain in a sympathetic union with Him in the state in which we have contemplated Him. This disposition of ours should not be allowed to lose its hold on us once we have quitted prayer; during the whole day, we should from time to time retrace in our memory the image of Our Lord as we saw Him in the morning's meditation. And when the moment of reducing to practice the good resolutions we have made presents itself, this mental picture will be of great assistance to us in exercising the act of virtue required.

Besides those acts of the will which arise naturally out of the subject, there are others which should form, as it were, the web on which should be woven the pattern of our intercourse with God. These we shall now consider.

CHAPTER XIII

"My heart and my flesh have rejoiced in the living God."
Ps. lxxxiii. 3.

*Development of Prayer : Meditation, Affective Prayer,
Prayer of Simplicity.*

IN the previous chapter were briefly outlined the acts which ordinarily constitute the body of prayer. Now besides those considerations and affections which are immediately concerned with the subject considered, there are certain movements of will and intellect which should interpenetrate all our relations with God in much the same way as a fundamental theme runs through all the figures of a piece of music. In all our interchanges of thought and affection with God, we must ever have before our eyes our sinfulness and infidelity. That we have sinned, and that, in spite of the extraordinary graces bestowed on us, we find it possible still, even daily, to fail in the duties of friendship towards our Heavenly Lord, is a fact that we must never lose sight of; it should impart a certain reserve to our warmest feelings or expressions of affection. Our love for God must be ever tinged with a sadness arising from the consciousness of our unworthiness to present ourselves before Him. We must never cast ourselves at His Feet to worship, without recalling that our worship must ascend to Him from hearts that to some degree have disappointed and wounded Him.

This thought will generate an ever present feeling of compunction without which there cannot be true devotion. This abiding sorrow for sin develops a sensitiveness to the claims of God on us; the nearer we approach to Him, the clearer grows the understanding that those claims cannot be satisfied without sanctity on our part. This helps to maintain us in a humble and subdued frame of mind, checks all tendency to presumptuous familiarity in our attitude towards our Creator, and effectively curbs all movements of self-will, vanity and uncharitableness. "And my sin is always before me," says Scripture.[1]

Through all our meditations there should run implicitly this spiritual confession. It should consist rather in a repentant attitude of the soul with regard to all its sins in general, than in a calling up for avowal any of them in particular. When the activities of thought and affection belonging to the main theme cease, the activities proper to this spiritual confession should emerge into prominence. They are a consideration of our guilt before, and ingratitude towards, God : regret that our sorrow is so imperfect and so wanting in divine love : a desire that we should have a truly humble and contrite heart, and a yearning for pardon and for the grace of amendment ; and all this should be accompanied by a longing to make atonement by sacrifice.

But whilst being filled with regret for our transgressions and shame for our unworthiness, we must never allow ourselves to lose sight of the graces and favours which God has bestowed on us. It would be a perverse form of humility to blind oneself to the good wrought in our soul by the action of divine grace.

[1] Ps. l. 5.

Profound gratitude for the favours God has bestowed on us should colour all our implicit pleadings for growth in virtue and holiness: "Bless the Lord O my soul, and never forget all He hath done for thee."[2] Many spend their spiritual energies in perpetually bewailing their sinfulness and do not allow themselves to advert to the truth that they have much to be grateful for—even spiritually. God likes us to bear in mind with gratitude how much He has done for us and with what loving care He watches over our spiritual welfare. With all our faults there are many graces which we have turned to profit. "To make open avowal of what I have received is not pride but devotion," says St. Augustine.[3] The smallest grace is of a value, St. Thomas tells us, that outweighs all the good of the whole created universe; and to arrive at that state in which one is privileged to converse intimately with God there is required a series of special graces which are not given to all. Those who have made even a little progress in the interior life could not exaggerate in their expressions of gratitude to Almighty God. That they, in preference to so many others, should be objects of that special providence by which they have been initiated into the life of prayer—of familiar intercourse with the Lord Himself—is a mystery, the mystery of Predestination. Their hearts should overflow with gratitude in face of this mystery of election. There are numbers of Christians around about them given the same opportunities as they, perhaps more deserving than they are, oftentimes endowed with much finer natural disposition, who are, nevertheless, destined to remain

[2] Ps. cii. 2.   [3] Comm. on Pater Noster.

during their whole life only on the borders of the supernatural world. Those who have made some progress have only to contrast their present dispositions with those they had when, as St. Paul puts it, they " were serving under the elements of the world ",⁴ to realise what freedom they have acquired and how good God has been to them. Feelings of deep gratitude towards God should be ever welling up in our hearts. Our sorrow for sin should not make us gloomy ; it should leave room for these feelings of joyous gratitude for what God has made us by His grace. This sense of gratitude, so far from marring humility, is an element of it. When the soul has, by frequent exercise, so strongly impregnated its ordinary method of prayer with the affections we have outlined that they come to predominate, then a change that is gradual and yet easily perceptible begins to make itself felt in our meditation. The soul has now become penetrated through and through with an affective knowledge of the mysteries of faith. It moves habitually in a supernatural atmosphere. Instinctively it considers everything from the spiritual point of view, that is, it sees, in the light of faith, the circumstances in which itself and those around it move. The assaults of its lower nature and of the passions have become enfeebled, and it no longer experiences a difficulty in directing its thoughts and affections towards God. In a word, the hold that the things of earth have had on it is relaxed and it feels a real attraction for God, and the things of God.

Meditation is still necessary for the soul when in this condition, but considerations and reflections now

⁴ Gal. iv. 3.

play a very minor part in this exercise. The ordinary
subjects chosen are still taken from the life of Our
Lord, or deal with the Christian virtues, studied in
themselves or as seen in exercise in His life or in the lives
of Our Blessed Lady and of His Saints. But no activity
of the reasoning powers is required to persuade the
soul of the necessity of practising those virtues; nor
is any activity of the imagination required to beget
an attraction for them. The soul habitually aspires
after perfection which it realises to be a condition of
close friendship with Jesus. Prayer, therefore, becomes
extremely simplified. A few thoughts having reference
to the spiritual life are taken to occupy the intelligence
and imagination, because this is a means that it is
necessary to take in order to enter into a state of recollection. One act of reflection is made on those ideas,
one glance, as it were, of the intelligence, when the
exercise begins and the whole soul, without any effort,
persuasion or reflection, is possessed of the truth which
they contain. Instantly the will, without feeling any
contrary appeal or counter attraction, is drawn to desire
with all its strength that perfection of life which the
living of those truths would mean. It does not seek that
perfection as an end, but as a means of making its union
with God more intimate. Though the soul knows that
it will fail when the time for action comes, still, at the
actual moment at any rate, it enters into a state of conformity in mind and heart and volition with the truth
it has meditated on. In this state of conformity it places
itself directly and deliberately under the action of God,
with a view to receiving into itself the outpouring of
that grace which will enable it later on to shape its

conduct according to the truth which it is contemplating. This prayer is called affective prayer because the acts of the intelligence being simple and rapid, the acts of the will, called affections, predominate. The prayer of affection, which is the ordinary development of prayer in souls who are generous, may receive a further simplification. The affections themselves cease to be multiple and varied and tend to unity. In this prayer the soul recollects all its powers. It stills their activity and throws all its being, and all the energies of that being, into a calm, simple, loving look directed to God. All multiplicity in the acts of the will gradually disappears. From time to time it elicits acts of love and of desire to be nearer to God—acts of aspiration after that union which it feels to be yet so far off. These acts of love are made without vehemence; they are more like the breathing of the soul than positive acts. They are almost mere pulsations. They resemble the slight heaving of the ocean when it has subsided into a relative calm.

The sense of the remoteness of its objective, namely, a very close union with God, provokes a longing in the soul which is a strange mingling of distress and contentment. Union with God is discerned to be far off and utterly unattainable by any efforts that the creature can make. It is clearly recognised to be a divine and gratuitous gift. It is impossible to know how it will be imparted and when. The soul recognises that a still more thorough transformation must take place in itself before deep and intimate union becomes possible, and yet it is only too well aware that no efforts of its own, however praiseworthy, can effect that transformation. The soul sees in a certain sense in what consists this perfection to which it aspires, but does not know how it can ever attain to it. All this causes a certain anxiety in its patient longing. But in its expectancy there is no sadness, it is content to hold itself before the Lord in a humble attitude of dumb pleading. Knowing that the Holy Ghost alone can purify it, it offers itself to His Divine operations, keeping itself silent and recollected and labouring to divest itself of all that could present an obstacle to the operations of the Divine Spirit. It does nothing but submit itself to the action of God. This is the prayer of simplicity. It is not without its inconveniences ; for those who have attained to it, oftentimes do not understand their own state. Finding in themselves a cessation of considerations and of distinct movements of the will, they think that they are doing nothing in prayer. The whole exercise takes place in the obscurity of faith ; hence there is little for the imagination to fix itself on, or anything to keep the understanding in activity. As a consequence distractions are very frequent, though the distractions are only apparent. The regard of the soul remains all the time fixed in God, while the images that rise in the imagination may even set the understanding in motion and draw it away to alien topics.[5]

[5] Bossuet describes very accurately the characteristics of the prayer of simplicity. "The greater its (the soul's) knowledge of God is, the purer will be its love, the more upright its intention, the more pronounced its hatred for sin, the more thorough its recollection, the more sustained its humility and mortification. . . . The light of faith grown stronger reveals to us our least imperfection and enables us to conceive a deep regret for them combined with a strong aversion from them. . . .

"The best prayer is that in which one most completely abandons oneself to the sentiments and dispositions that God puts into the soul and in which one strives simply, with humility, candour and fidelity to conform oneself to His will and to the example of Jesus Christ." Bossuet : *Prayer of Simplicity*.

"The Prayer of Simplicity ", says Fr. Poulain, " is a mental prayer in

But on the whole the soul enjoys a great measure of peace when it has passed the stage of ordinary meditation and entered into that of affective prayer, or the Prayer of Simplicity. It is not unaware, in spite of its consciousness of its utter weakness and powerlessness for good, that a great revolution has taken place in itself, a revolution which it recognises by its effects. It lives in the sense of God's pervading presence, and in the perception of God's action on it through creatures. The gradual deepening of its faith, has put it in contact with the reality underlying the external aspect of created objects. It is no longer led away by appearances: the transitoriness of things has come home to it:— external, sensible objects though still capable of soliciting, have lost their power over its affections. Gradually, everything has dissolved and left it face to face with the only reality, God Himself. It has been brought to God the Father through meditation on the mystery of the Incarnation. "No man cometh to the Father but by Me."[6] God has become for it the supreme reality; life holds for it no other, except what brings it into relation to Him; existence without Him means nothing and holds out no prospect. Life empty of God is empty of everything and the thought of such a life inspires it

which (1) intuition in a great measure replaces reasoning; (2) the affections and resolutions show very little variety and are expressed in few words. . . . In the prayer of simplicity there is a thought or a sentiment that returns incessantly and easily (although with little or no development) amongst many other thoughts, whether useful or not. This dominant thought does not go so far as to be continuous. It merely returns frequently and of its own accord. We may compare it to . . . a piece of wood which, carried along by a torrent, continually goes under the surface, disappears and reappears." *The Grace of Interior Prayer*, Ch. ii. Republished by C.T.S.E. under the title: *Prayer of Simplicity*.

[6] "Nemo venit ad Patrem nisi per me." St. John xiv. 6.

with horror. As the compass needle trembles, wavers and is agitated, being drawn in different directions until it finally steadies itself and takes up its definite position under the force of magnetic attraction, so the soul ceases its vacillations at this stage and steadily points towards God.

The end is not yet; but the soul looks forward confidently to that consummation. As Faith grows in strength and vigour the theological virtue of Hope develops with it. And acting under the influence of that virtue, the soul, in spite of its nothingness and its deep sense of that nothingness, looks forward with confidence to the moment when God will stoop to it, lessen the distance that separates it from Him, and impart to it an increasingly perfect union with Himself, and, if He so will, carry it from the state of active into that of passive prayer.

PART III

ELEMENTS THAT MAKE FOR PROGRESS
IN MENTAL PRAYER

ELEMENTS THAT MAKE FOR PROGRESS
IN MENTAL PRAYER

CHAPTER XIV

DISPOSITIONS REQUISITE FOR MENTAL PRAYER

*" If I have looked at iniquity in my heart, the Lord
will not hear me."*—Ps. lxv. 18.

§1. Purity of Conscience.

SINCE prayer is a relation of intimate friendship
with One Who is infinitely holy, progress in
it demands a great purity of conscience. The soul
must not be content with merely cleansing itself from
grievous faults, it must aim at preserving a deep aversion
for every deliberate venial sin. Faults of weakness it cannot
escape, but everything wilful should be carefully avoided.
When there is absent this delicacy in one's relations with
Almighty God, it is a sign that the exercise of prayer does
not touch the depths of the soul where contact with God
is found ; because where such contact exists, it is impossible not to feel sharp stings of remorse for every action
which consciously deviates from the will of God, even
though it be but to the extent of not co-operating with it.

§2. Purity of Heart.

It is our irregular and inordinate affections for persons
or things that alone lead us into deliberate faults.
Hence it is that it becomes incumbent on us to labour

to purify our affections. It is most important to aim at
loving only God, and severing every tie of which the
Divine Master is not the beginning and the end. Our
Lord Who has created our human hearts, does not dis-
countenance the natural affections of those hearts ;
on the contrary, He consecrates and blesses all. It is
only when they become disorderly and usurp the place
of God, in our souls, that they become displeasing to
Him. The soul desirous of progress must aim then,
not at destroying its natural affections, but rather at
purifying them. It must make its object be to love only
according to God, and in the manner in which He
approves. The instant that it finds any attachment
causing its relations with God to cool, or making it feel
uncomfortable and ill at ease in His presence, it must bring
such an attachment to an abrupt termination. It is the only
remedy ; one must be drastic in this matter. As long as the
soul is attached inordinately to anything created, it has no
longer the same freedom as before to raise itself up to
God. A nothing can keep it tied to earth, and God
dwells only in heaven. There our affections ought to be.[1]

§3. Purity of Mind.

To live in a state of prayer demands that the mind
be constantly occupied with the thought of God. This
does not mean that the entire day be spent in the
exercise of meditation. This is impossible. It means
simply that all our actions should at least subconsciously
be guided and influenced by a sense of God's Sovereignty.

[1] " Does it make any difference," says St. John of the Cross, " whether
a bird be held by a slender thread or by a rope, while the bird is bound it
cannot fly 'till the cord that holds it is broken ? " *Ascent* I. xi.

This postulates a control by the will over the workings of the mind and, consequently, over the activity of the imagination. Our trains of thought are governed from within or from without. If from within they are under the sway of the will and can be made to issue from considerations of faith; if from without, they are under the sway of nature. Things impress the imagination, the images of the imagination start the processes of thought, and these processes follow the course set by the images of the inferior faculty. Hence if we allow outside things that have no bearing on the life for God, to occupy our imagination and fill it, reflection on spiritual matters becomes exceedingly difficult. Dissipation and distraction are the natural consequence of allowing the imagination to occupy itself with images that have no connection with the higher life. To abandon oneself habitually to every caprice of one's mind, to make no effort to be master of one's mental activities, no effort to direct them at one's will, and at the same time to expect to lead an interior life, is to expect what cannot be realised. "Purity," says St. Thomas, "is necessary if the mind is to be applied to God, because the human mind is sullied when it is attached to inferior things; just as anything is rendered impure by being mixed with something baser, e.g. silver when mixed with lead. The mind ought to be withdrawn from inferior objects if it is to be united to the supreme object; and therefore the mind that lacks purity cannot be applied to God."[2]

---

[2] "Munditia enim necessaria est ad hoc quod mens Deo applicetur, quia mens humana inquinatur ex hoc quod inferioribus rebus conjungitur; sicut quaelibet res ex immixtione pejoris sordescit, ut argentum ex immixtione plumbi. Oportet autem quod mens ab inferioribus rebus abstrahatur, ad

§4. Purity of Will.

The faculties of thought and imagination being emancipated from the control of creatures, and subjected to the control of the will, one must set about the purification of this latter faculty. The will is the faculty by which we move towards and cleave to what is presented to us as being good, that is, as satisfying a want in us. Whilst depending on the intelligence for its object, the will, in virtue of the freedom that is inherent in it, can control that faculty. The will is purified when it seeks only God and the things that pertain to God, amongst which is its own spiritual perfection or its own union with the divinity. To attain this state of purity it must employ its liberty to cause the intellect to judge as " good " only that which brings us to God. Its purification, therefore, consists in the gradual elimination from its tendencies of all that is not God or does not lead directly to Him. Thus it attains its perfection in an unquestioning submission to the action of Divine Providence, and in embracing wholeheartedly the dispensations of that Providence in the minutest details of life. The purity of the will leads to the taking of strong and efficacious resolutions.

§5. Strong Devotion.

This is based upon a deep realisation of God's absolute sovereignty over us, and His right to unqualified

---

hoc quod supremae rei possit conjungi; et ideo mens sine munditia Deo applicarti non potest." (II. II. Q.81. a.8.)

subjection on our part; and it means a promptitude of
disposition to obey Him in all things and to exhibit
a great generosity in His service.[3] The soul possessed
of true devotion is not content merely with carrying
out God's orders, it aims at forestalling His wishes.
Devotedness is something far higher than mere duty.
It is inventive to discover ways of giving pleasure to
the Person, who is its object. Great projects planned
and undertaken for the promotion of God's cause
find their inspiration in devotion. Sometimes it is
accompanied by a certain sweetness and suavity which
sustains this promptitude of the will and permeates
the soul with a relish for the things of God. But this
is purely accidental to devotion. More often, devotion
is exercised without any feeling of relish and in the
darkness of faith; this absence of feeling is called spiritual
dryness. For faithful souls, such dryness is a test
of their sincerity and a trial sent by God to purify and
deepen their faith. For the more the soul acts by the
prompting of faith alone, unsustained by any help
coming from its sensible feelings and emotions, the
more perfect that faith becomes. But for souls that are
less strong and not so advanced, the absence of sensible
devotion may easily be the consequence of immortification and slight but continued infidelities. If the soul,
losing courage because no longer finding satisfaction
in serving God, ceases to make efforts to acquire obedience, forbearance and humility, it loses not only the
sweetness of devotion but devotion itself. If, however,
it does what it can to remain united to God, even though

---

[3] "Devotion," says St. Thomas, "is the will to give oneself with
promptitude to the things that belong to the service of God." (II. II. 82. 1.)

it can hardly succeed in so doing, it has preserved devotion substantially.

§6. Knowledge of Self.

It is most important to have some knowledge of self, of our own tendencies, of our weaknesses and of our qualities. Blindness as to what we really are, can prove a great obstacle to our progress : for it will lead to continual mistakes as to what in us proceeds from nature and what from grace. Through such blindness we may easily be resisting the instincts and the promptings of the Holy Ghost, Who usually directs us in accordance with our natural aptitudes. This self-knowledge should never degenerate into minute self-analysis : that would prove just as harmful as ignorance. It is best acquired by the exercise of humility and by striving to live habitually in the presence of God. Self-revelation comes very slowly, because the more deeply rooted our own tendencies are, the more they form part of ourselves and as a consequence the less they obtrude themselves on our notice when we enter on action. We are less a mystery to others than to ourselves. This is the psychological reason for the need of spiritual direction. It is also the reason why we can so easily discern the mote in another's eye and be blind to the beam in our own.

§7. The Christian Motive.

Our Divine Lord's infinite wisdom is wonderfully reflected in his admonition : " Lay up to yourselves

treasures in heaven . . . for where thy treasure is,
there is thy heart also ".[4] Our interests and affections
naturally govern our life and its activities. To succeed
in the spiritual life, it is necessary for us to labour to
place our affections at the service of our faith. Attachments are our great obstacle. The readiest means to
overcome them is, not to turn in on ourselves to combat
them directly, for sooner or later we would lose in the
struggle, but to turn outward and upward and combat
them indirectly by creating counter attachments, in
the spiritual order. Progress will necessarily be slow
for us as long as our emotions are at variance with the
dictates of our faith. To make our course easier, it
will be necessary to effect a union between the two.
The purely spiritual, because it is such, makes little or
no appeal to our sensibility. Something must be sought
out between God and our soul, which may serve as
a lever to lift us above the earth and bring us as it were
into God's reach. This lever must contain elements that,
whilst giving free exercise to our senses, our feelings,
and our imagination, still tend to carry us on to God and
to bring us into relations with Him. The grandeur
of the catholic liturgy is such a thing that standing as it
were midway between the sensible and the spiritual
world, effects a union between the two by supernatural-
ising the former. Our senses, purified and refined by
the expressive and beautiful symbolic vesture in which
holy Church robes the deeply spiritual mysteries of
our religion, will by this discipline satisfy and elevate
the sensibility and thus develop the emotional tendencies
in perfect harmony with the ultimate aspirations of the

[4] St. Matt. vi. 20-21.

human soul. This harmony being established between the tendencies of sense and spirit, the soul will be free from that which presents the greatest obstacle to its supernatural development, namely, the opposition to our soul's upward movement which arises from our sensitive nature craving for satisfactions that must be denied it, if purity of heart and conscience is to be preserved. Through the appeal of the Church's ritual, we shall be drawn into a sympathy with the mind of the Church which has created that ritual for its outward expression. Drawn into the current of the life of the Church, the soul will begin to breathe easily, as it were, in the supernatural world. That world becomes its connatural element. In it, it will become gradually penetrated through and through with the atmosphere that prevails there. The life of the Church manifests itself uniquely in the love of its Divine Spouse, Jesus Christ. Every act of the Sacred Liturgy, every ceremony, every expression is dictated by that love, has its source in it, and is the means by which that love finds voice and utterance. The soul that is in sympathy with, and which enters into this liturgical life, gradually assimilates that enthusiastic love of Jesus Christ, with which the Church palpitates. In this pure and spiritual love the soul goes outside of itself, relinquishes itself, and espouses the interests of its Beloved. It makes its own the interests of Jesus Christ and those of His Church, which are identical. These interests are simply one absorbing interest, the salvation of the souls of men. This zeal for the expansion of the Church, this consuming desire to bring ever increasing numbers into its fold, becomes the 'grande passion' of the soul that is seized by the spirit of the sacred Liturgy. The soul that is possessed by it finds therein the great lever by which it is lifted up above that preoccupation about self which is the chief obstacle to progress. In this selflessness it will find that quality of simplicity which Jesus so admired in children, and which He postulated as the condition of entrance into the kingdom of heaven. The kingdom of heaven is realised for us here on earth, in close and intimate union with God.

CHAPTER XV

§1. A Preparation for Meditation

" Thy word is a lamp to my feet and a light to my paths."—Ps. cxviii. 105.

SAINT AUGUSTINE says that " he who wishes often to be with God ought to pray frequently and read pious books," and all spiritual writers after him, without exception, have insisted on the necessity of spiritual reading for all those who wish to lead a really interior and supernatural life.[1] Holiness is the fruit of prayer, and mental prayer is extremely difficult without the reading of spiritual books. Such reading provides the foundation on which the work of meditation is to be built up; it affords an immediate preparation for the exercise and ministers the element by which it is to be sustained. It is to the exercise of prayer what oil is to the lamp; it supplies the material from which the flame of fervour derives its nourishment and by which it is kept bright and burning. It is for this reason that

---

[1] To quote a few examples from the Doctors of the Church : St. Bernard in his explanation of the words, " seek and you shall find," says, " Seek in reading and you shall find in meditation. Strike by your prayers and the door of contemplation shall be flung open ". St. Jerome wrote to Saline, " Spiritual reading is a sovereign remedy against evil thoughts ", while St. Augustine says, " Reading the scripture is like reading letters from the other world ".

We know also that the conversion of several saints began in spiritual reading. The best known example is that of St. Ignatius, who was prompted to change his manner of life and give himself wholly to God because of his attentive perusal of a spiritual book, during convalescence. On the other hand the progress in perfection of St. Jerome (who otherwise led a very austere life) was retarded because of his zeal for pagan authors. (See Scaramelli : *Direct Ascet.*, Art. iv.)

the religious orders from the beginning have insisted
so much on the necessity of spiritual reading, making
it a point of rule, and taking every precaution against
the disregard or neglect of it. St. Benedict appointed
two monks to go round the Monastery at a fixed hour
to see that everybody was " making " his spiritual
reading, and St. Ignatius writes in his rules: " The
religious should twice a day employ (therein) the
time allotted, for examination of conscience, for meditation and spiritual reading; and with all possible care
and diligence apply themselves thereunto in the Lord".
It is a matter to be regretted that this devotional exercise
is confined mostly to those who have given themselves to the religious life, and that books dealing
with the characteristics and lives of the saints, as well
as with the principles and laws of the life of union
with God find a place in few libraries except those of
religious houses. They should find a place on the book-
shelves of every truly christian home.

All are called to perfection, to that grade of perfection
which consists in conformity with the law of the Gospel,
and this cannot be attained without constant and intimate
union with Our Divine Lord. For this union spiritual
reading forms an almost indispensable condition. The
reason is obvious. Prayer being an elevation of our
souls to God, and this elevation consisting in acts of
the understanding and movements of the will, it is
plain that our souls must be as it were steeped in a
supernatural element, in order that they may easily
and readily ascend to God. If our minds are not familiar
with divine things this elevation of the soul will be very
difficult. The extent of our familiarity with the super-

natural will be the measure of the facility which we shall find in giving ourselves to prayer. Of course this facility depends on more than mere knowledge of spiritual books and our own efforts when we give ourselves to prayer. Even when we have done all that is required on our part, the results may still be poor, for in each case, the successful accomplishment of the exercise of mental prayer is a grace and a gift from God. But although God may also impart knowledge of divine things directly, without the intermediary of books, this is not in accord with the ordinary procedure of His Providential guidance of souls. His grace is meant not to supersede but to raise and elevate nature. He does not as a rule interfere with the regular working of natural laws. The ordinary modes by which new ideas come to our minds are reading and instruction. As our minds are constituted they dwell easily and naturally on those thoughts with which they are stored, and which have the most interest for us. If worldly pursuits, worldly interests, mere natural and material things absorb our attention, and are the main theme of such reading as we indulge in, it is inevitable that our reflections will take the colour of these preoccupations and interests when we set ourselves to prayer. It is according to the laws of psychology that in such circumstances our thoughts will tend to run almost entirely on earthly things, things quite foreign to prayer. Our best attempts will issue simply in endless distractions, in virtue of the laws that govern the workings of the human mind. Prayer is not a haphazard thing nor can it issue from the best will in the world unless we take account of the lines on which our minds are constructed and adopt our

measures in view of this structure and according to
the direction it imposes. If we wish to dwell easily
on supernatural things our memories must be stored
with them.

Saintliness is an art; it is always the product of
adhesion to certain principles, and is the application
of these principles in the conduct of life.[2] If we follow
certain methods of action we can become saints, but only
on condition that we do follow these methods. If a
man wishes to acquire an art he gives himself to a certain
well-defined course of training, and to the learning of
a code of rules. His success will depend on his assiduity
and application. In the same way sanctity is a methodical
affair and is never an accident.[3] Now meditation is
the introduction to a devout life, and meditation, being
a work of the mind, presents grave obstacles unless
the mind is equipped for it. The Gospel is the text
book of sanctity. For this reason our intelligence must
be habituated to the examples of the Gospel by continually dwelling on them. The text of the Gospel
receives its illustration and amplification in works
dealing with the lives of the Saints and with spiritual
themes. Spiritual reading has no other purpose than

---

[2] Saint Catherine of Siena in her dialogue returns on this point more
than once, namely, that sanctity is the outcome of the actions and reactions
that follow relations with one's fellow-creatures. When these actions and
reactions are governed by the principle of divine charity and follow the
lines traced by Jesus Christ in His life, then sanctity is attained.

[3] Art is the right procedure as determined by reason that is to be followed,
if one's efforts are to issue in work that is perfect, in cases where the work
proceeds from the human brain and hand. Ars est recta ratio factibilium.
In a similar way there is an art of sanctity. It is the procedure that is to be
followed in our spiritual, mental and moral activities, if sanctity is to result
from these activities. A Saint is a moral work of art, a finished product
of personally controlled and personally directed actions. The art of sanctity
has its fixed principles as have the fine arts.

to store our minds with ideas and our imaginations with images pertaining to the supernatural order. And since our minds dwell with ease and for a length of time only on what interests them, the daily reading of pious books must not be merely an exercise to be got through, but a pursuit to which we assiduously devote ourselves. It will entirely fail of its purpose unless it gives a certain very definite turn to our thoughts and a particular trend to our minds. It should extend its influence beyond the mere space of time which is allotted to it ; the manner in which we form our judgments about things and devote ourselves to the occupations of our lives must be largely influenced by it. It is only when understood in this way that it forms a valuable aid to mental prayer. For when the tone of our mind is supernaturalised little difficulty will be experienced in putting ourselves in the proper attitude of soul whenever we place ourselves in the presence of God for the formal exercise of prayer.[4] All the difference between the ability and the inability to pray lies in living or in not living the life of faith.[5] The life of faith consists in thinking and acting with a view to God and estimating the things of this world after the manner of the Saints. If our reading is done with ardour, with a mind that is open to receive the impressions that spiritual books of themselves necessarily convey, we shall gradually form

[4] The immediate end of spiritual reading is the elevation of mind and heart to God, and the removal of opposing obstacles. It is really then a way of making prayer ; and on that account is of capital importance both for the christian and for the religious life. " This exercise is one of very great importance," says St. Eudes, " and operates in the soul the same effects as mental prayer." (La Lecture Spirituelle." J. Gauderon in *La Vie Spirituelle*, June, 1921, p. 186.)

[5] Cf. chaps. vi and x.

the habit of thinking in a supernatural way. Once this habit is formed, the chief and greatest obstacle to the interior life is swept away.

It is not an easy thing for us to think supernaturally, and an occasional look into a spiritual book will not be sufficient to develop in us the habit of doing so. If we are to keep our judgments sure in a spiritual sense, our outlook on life wise with true wisdom, and our conduct under the guidance and control of motives of faith as opposed to those of worldliness, spiritual reading must come to form the most substantial element in our daily intellectual nourishment. It is only thus that it will effectively counterbalance the evil tendencies of nature by awakening and sustaining supernatural tendencies in the soul. Spiritual reading substitutes for the maxims and examples of the world, the maxims and examples of Our Lord and the Saints. In a word, it is a kind of daily invitation to look beyond earth to God and the things of God.[6] It must not be the least important, but the most important part of our reading. This does not mean that we are to open none but ascetical works—no, but it means that the impressions or cast of thought that we derive from the reading of these must determine, control and correct the cast of thought that our ordinary reading tends naturally to produce. Our estimate of the ideas that are enunciated or adumbrated in the secular books must be guided and checked by the principles laid down by spiritual authors and not vice versa. This is most necessary if we are to set up an effective barrier to the stream of worldliness

[6] (" La Lecture Spirituelle." J. Gauderon in *La Vie Spirituelle*, June. 1921, p. 186.)

that is pouring in on us from every side. Our duties
may necessitate that a great part of our time for reading
will be given to the perusal of books that are frankly
humanistic and unspiritual in tendency, that are purely
materialistic in outlook and that value life in accordance
with the sum of purely earthly happiness and well-being
that it can furnish. Constant reading of these, especially
when they are written in an attractive style, and with a
certain force and plausibility of argument, will introduce
their subtle poison into our minds unless we are careful
to apply the antidote of spiritual reading. Furthermore,
Christians are obliged to live and move in an atmosphere
saturated with worldliness, in a world in which almost
every appreciation of things is at variance with the
appreciations of Jesus Christ, and their judgments
cannot remain unaffected by the prevailing tone and
tendency of the environment unless a steady corrective
be applied. This corrective is to be found in the use of
spiritual books. The baneful spirit of naturalism is
nowadays not restricted to a definite number or confined
to particular regions: it pervades the whole world.
To-day, the words of St. Paul find an almost literal
verification: " for all seek the things that are their
own, not the things that are Jesus Christ's ".[7] The
doors of no Christian home can be barred so securely,
the walls of no religious house can be raised so high,
as to shut out this perverse, anti-gospel spirit. It
penetrates with its subtle poison everywhere. Its
influence is felt within the best Christian communities.
Selfishness is becoming a code of conduct; and men
use their genius to discover and bring forward reasons

[7] Phil. ii. 21.

and establish principles that justify their self-seeking.
The gospel of the world formulates its own beatitudes,
which are faithfully echoed by those who pass as
normally good Christians. In unison with the worldling
they say : " Blessed are they that have a good time ".
" Blessed are they that have enough of wealth to satisfy
every whim ". " Blessed are they that can have their
own way in all things and can crush opposition ", etc.
" Self-sacrifice, " the world says, " was all right for men
who lived at a time when men could not know any
better—people are too enlightened nowadays to entertain any longer these mediæval ideas of perfection."
The air we breathe is reeking with these poisonous
thought-germs which tend to destroy the spiritual life
of the soul ; for it substitutes a narrow, selfish and hard
calculation for the childlike trust in a loving Providence
so recommended by the Gospel.

Apart from all these adverse influences that come
from the world we should still find enough of difficulty
in ourselves, enough of obstacles to the formation of
supernatural habits of thought. Nothing reveals itself
to our consciousness in normal conditions but what is
of the natural order. We have no power of discriminating
by mere consciousness between what is a natural and
what is a supernatural act in ourselves. In fact the
supernaturalness of any act of faith or hope or charity
that we elicit can never be revealed to our consciousness
except, perhaps, in the highest mystical states. If we
go back over any of the processes by which God
stirred our soul in a special manner at any period of
our lives, they will appear to us to resemble any other
processes of thought or emotion, differing only in regard

of the matter with which they are concerned. We assign the change wrought in ourselves to the eloquence of the preacher, the arguments he used, the clear and vivid way in which he put truths we had often heard before, etc. In a word, the whole thing took place, we think, in a way which we can explain, by the ordinary laws of cause and effect. It is only one that is skilled in interior things that can detect the presence of divine grace operating in all these things, and without the operation of which, they would have proved ineffectual. There is, then, a decided tendency in us to look at things and judge of them in a purely natural manner.

Now spiritual reading alone, which puts us in touch with and makes us acquainted with the temper of the Saints, with their habits of thought, with their estimate of things, will succeed in counteracting all these influences, and give a certain insight into the action of God in life's happenings. Association with the Saints through spiritual reading forms and strengthens in us the conviction that the one thing of supreme value is, not to be well off in this world, but to be well established in the state of grace, to be well with God; that all the world's goods without the friendship of God are valueless, and that sanctifying grace even without these goods is sufficient; that the contemplation of divine things is a more energetic influence than feverish activity; that the accomplishment of God's will and not the gratification of our own is the chief business of life; and that a man's greatness consists not in wealth or power or honour, but in that degree of divine charity with which his soul is informed.

§2. What we are to Read

If the works of ascetical writers are necessary in order to give us a good grasp of the science of spirituality, it is the lives of the Saints that will give us the stimulus to put what we know in practice. What is concrete appeals to us more readily than what is abstract—and in the lives of these heroic men and women we see christian principles in actual working. Without the records of their lives before us, the life of christian perfection as portrayed in the Gospel would run the danger of appearing to our weakness as an ideal impossible to realise, the evangelical counsels and the teaching of the Lord Jesus would appear as something to admire rather than to practise, and, our natural weakness aiding, the teaching of the Saviour would soon lose all practical hold upon our hearts and wills. In the lives of the Saints we have positive evidence that perfection is attainable—and that what is impossible to human nature by itself, becomes possible and is actually realised through the grace of Jesus Christ. These records of the lives of these heroic men and women show that all that is required on our part in order to reach sanctity is humility and the entire submission to the Holy Will of God; they show that when these dispositions of humility and fidelity to the divine will are contributed by man, with the help of grace, the divine action can make the rarest virtues grow and flourish in the soul. The reading of the lives of the Saints saves us from the danger of believing that the gospel outlines an ideal which is practically impossible.

There is another danger from which Spiritual reading preserves us—a danger into which many fall, and which has proved a stumbling block to them on the road to perfection. The danger lies in this. The morality taught by Our Lord is so lofty and so uncompromisingly opposed to the inclinations of our lower nature that, under the promptings of that nature, we should be tempted to whittle down the sayings of the Divine Master, explain away their sense, elude their obvious meaning, prune them of all that is sharp and exacting and seek to give them an interpretation more in harmony with the pleasure-loving, easy, comfortable life which is our ambition. So great is our aversion to what is austere and difficult, so unresponsive are we to the appeal to mortification and self-sacrifice, that this tendency would be sure to manifest itself in us, even if there were question merely of the ordinary christian principles, and the counsels of perfection were left out of consideration. This tendency—to explain away the ' exactingness ' of the Gospel—is discernible universally in those who, through a total neglect of spiritual literature, are not conversant with the Saints and their ways, and it is evident also even in those who read the lives of the Saints but who do it in a perfunctory manner, or by way of a task. Such persons, judging things by the low standards set by their own lives, are inclined to say, in face of the inexorable morality of the Gospel—" Such and such a principle or maxim of conduct must not be taken in the strict sense ". " Putting such principles in practice life would be impossible." " No man could live in the manner required by such a rule." With the example of thousands and tens of thousands of saints, of all ages, of all nations, of all ranks and of both sexes, before our eyes, such questionings are silenced. Christian perfection is possible because so many, even of the tenderest age, mere boys and girls, as for instance St. Pancratius and St. Agnes, have attained to it. In their lives we see in actual working, intense love of God, ardent love of the neighbour, a great spirit of self-denial and an eminent degree of the exercise of the moral and the theological virtues.

There is no one but recognises the force of example. Any amount of instruction may fail to rouse to stern endeavour the sluggish, those who are not naturally of an elevated, noble or generous temperament. But when the instruction is embodied in a life, which is its living expression, then even the dullest are aroused to energetic action. A great and good life excites admiration in the hearts of all that contemplate it. Admiration begets imitation. We have an inborn tendency to assume the ways and manners of those we admire. Hence it is that books written for boys deal mostly with the doings of the chief character, who is pictured as possessing all the qualities that it is desired should be emulated by the youthful reader, viz :—truthfulness, honesty, fair dealing, judgment and courage. These ideal figures fire the imagination, and the boy reader is filled with the desire to resemble in all things the hero of his book. Reading of this kind plays a large part in forming the ideals of young boys and in determining their estimates of all that is great and heroic. Great harm then can be done, and is done, in setting before the young mind a false standard of manliness and virtue. One is naturally drawn to greatness, and if our idea of greatness is false, it is easy to see to what a perverted notion of what really constitutes a great and manly life a false standard may give rise. That man alone is truly great who is perfect in self-mastery, and who is perfectly submissive to Almighty God; this is the perfectly moral and religious man. It is the Saints only who have fully and adequately realised this ideal. We cannot have what is truly lofty and noble constantly before our thoughts without being drawn to make the effort to reproduce at least something of that loftiness and nobility in our own lives. This does not mean that we are to strive to imitate the personal characteristics or the heroic individual actions or mortifications of the Saints in our conduct. Imitation of the Saints does not mean copying them. The attempt would be futile and end only in caricature and finally in disappointment. We imitate them by shaping our lives according to the principles which governed theirs, and by accepting their practical estimation of things, and not necessarily in making our own the material circumstances and the actual doings of their lives. We are not called upon to do what they did aided by the particular graces that were given them. But we are called upon to judge things as they did and view life and its activities after their manner.

Many find spiritual reading distasteful and insipid. This will be the case especially for those who indulge overmuch or even to any serious degree in romantic literature. Even when the tone of this is not really bad it exercises a very disturbing effect on the imagination, and renders the assimilation of spiritual ideas difficult.

The sensuous always appeals to us more readily than the spiritual, and hence those eager to lead a truly interior life must exercise a rigid mortification in the matter of light literature. What is bad or of a dangerous tendency must be wholly shunned by all who aspire even to an ordinary christian life. It is unfortunate that parents and teachers do not understand how utterly unchristian can be the mentality created by the works to which they so readily give their approval, if they find nothing in them openly contrary to faith and morals. For those who aim at intimacy with God, the selection of recreative reading must be much more careful; everything taken into their hands with a view to affording mental relaxation should tend at the same time to elevate and ennoble the mind. Nothing should be provided which would only stimulate and excite the imagination. Books turning upon the interplay of human passions, and without any supernatural background to the dramatic representation of the loves and hates of mankind, vitiate the taste and take away all relish for books that deal with the spiritual experiences of those who have given themselves to the life of intercourse with God.

Books that derive all their charm from the vividness with which they portray the deep emotions of earthly and natural affection are dangerous for souls which have consecrated the love of their hearts to God. The heart of the priest and the nun must be virginal, and should be carefully shielded from everything that would excite in it an interest in the play of human passions. The imagination of those who, turning their back on secular life and renouncing by vow the joys of domestic life, have bound themselves to tend towards perfection, should, as far as depends on their efforts, be kept free from all images of profane love. Then again those who have not had the same call and who, having tasted the joys held out by the world, have experienced the bitterness and disillusionment which too often attends the experiment, will instinctively, in their revulsion of feeling, turn for comfort and consolation to souls consecrated to the service of God. Those who are disillusioned with life will trust to these consecrated souls to establish contact once more between themselves and the supernatural world, with which, in their worldly existence, they had gradually lost touch. If they, whose profession is an exclusive devotedness to the things of God, have nothing to offer to the world-weary ones who look to them for an uplifting, except those very maxims, principles, and views of the world which have proved so bitter a disillusionment, they will have betrayed the legitimate trust that has been reposed in them. Consecrated souls must keep in close touch with God, for the sake of others as well as in their own interest. They must be always prepared in mind and will to be a guide to the supernatural world, for those who are broken by the trials of earth; for it is to that super-natural world and the God Who reigns in it, that the human heart, when crushed under the burden of existence, will immediately turn for healing and hope, if once it has known the goodness of that God. If they, whose function it is to play the part of intermediary with God, allow their minds to be formed to the same pattern as the minds of those who live in habitual neglect of divine things: if they waste their time, dissipate their energies and enervate their imaginations with the same type of literature as fashions the taste and charms the leisure of the worldling, then they cannot fulfil satisfactorily what is expected of them. It is true that sometimes those who are devoting themselves seriously to the cultivation of an interior life, are obliged in the discharge of their duties to make an acquaintance with the books that are in vogue. But while doing this they should hold themselves well on their guard against the seduction of that reading and keep their literary taste pure and uncontaminated. Interior souls should beware of making the perusal of romantic literature a recreation: they should give themselves to it as to a task and regret the time that may have to be spent in it. Where possible an interior soul should renounce all indulgence in light or romantic literature. If one who desires to give himself to spirituality has not a taste for spiritual books, then that taste should be cultivated, for it can be acquired. Its acquisition is, according to Father Faber, clearly a sign of predestination; it is at any rate a powerful help towards a spiritual life. When our minds are by constant reading steeped in the thoughts of God and divine things, it will be easy for us to think of Him, and it will come natural and easy for us to speak to Him and to speak of Him out of our full hearts and well-stored minds.

After one is grounded deeply in spirituality it becomes possible to touch these works of fiction without being defiled; they will have lost their appeal; they will be read only through necessity; they will be read not for amusement but in order that one may be a service to and a guidance to others.

§3. How We are to Read

Spiritual reading as an aid to the development of an interior life is an exercise which bears a close affinity to actual prayer. It is not practised mainly in view of gaining knowledge about things spiritual. Its object is rather to stir up the affections than to equip the intelligence. Reading for curiosity and " devouring " page after page of spiritual works defeats the very purpose for which spiritual reading is undertaken. There is a wide difference between religious reading and that which is read as an immediate help to mental prayer. The end of religious reading is instruction and enlighten-ment. It is necessary especially for directors of souls who must, by reason of their office, acquire a profound and scientific knowledge of asceticism and spirituality. The study of mystical, dogmatic and moral theology is religious reading. It goes without saying that religious reading must be supplemented by that which is properly spiritual in the case of those who are charged with the direction of souls : without it their instructions will lack the unction that is discovered in the words only of those whose thoughts move habitually in the spiritual world. The mere exercise of the intellect on questions that concern the objects of faith does not, of itself, steep the soul in a supernatural atmosphere. The soul's being so steeped in divine things is, as was pointed out, a condition of facility in and growth in prayer. Spiritual reading is an invaluable aid to this, on condition that it is done in the proper way. Hurried and dilettante reading is to be deprecated. The books taken up should be read through : passing from one to the other, after having read a little in each, disturbs the calm and balance of the soul. A desire to have one's spirit drawn to and strongly attracted by all that belongs to the interior life should be the motive impulse in spiritual reading. As counselled by the Saints and masters of the interior life its purpose is to affect the heart and will, making them enamoured of heavenly things, of virtues, of divine grace, of purity of soul, of growth in intimacy with our Divine Lord. One must be very dull and miserable not to be powerfully drawn by the beauty of the world of grace as revealed in the soul confidences of the Saints. The characteristics of their intimate converse with God, their union with Jesus Christ, and the marvellous transforming and divinising effects wrought in their souls through this intimacy and this union must, if read in a true interior spirit, excite in the heart of the reader a desire to penetrate, were it for ever so little a space, into this world of happiness and of beauty.

That this be the effect, the reading, as has just been stated, must be made in a disposition akin to prayerfulness. One should read slowly allowing oneself plenty of time and allowing what is read to sink well into the mind, so that the intelligence be penetrated by the truths exposed in the text and the will strongly drawn towards them. " Read with attention and application of mind and heart," says St. John Eudes, " weighing, tasting and digesting at leisure the sense and the substance of the words."[8] If spiritual reading be hurried through natural curiosity to get through a great number

[8] *Royaume de Jesus :* Preface.

of books, it will do very little good indeed.[9] Reading
should begin with a fervent invocation of God and
should be interrupted and interspersed with pious aspirations or ejaculatory prayer. It should be selected in
view of one's actual spiritual condition and in accordance
with one's spiritual needs. Reading that has no connection
with the soul's tendencies at the moment cannot prove
very beneficial. That the exercise should yield its full
fruits, there should be a close and vital connection
between one's reading and one's mental prayer.

§4. How to Profit by the Lives of the Saints

"Be ye followers of me," says St. Paul, "as I am
of Christ."[10] The same indeed may be said of all the
Saints—they are our models in the way of Christian
perfection. It has been asserted with the falsity that
habitually marks statements that proceed from a desire
to appear clever rather than to express the truth, that
the Saints are rather objects of admiration than of
imitation. In canonising the heroes of the christian
warfare the Church invites the rest of her children
to walk in their footsteps. But by imitation is not
meant a slavish reproduction of the circumstances of
their lives, of their exceptional austerities, of their
personal characteristics and of all that was peculiarly
personal to them. This would be an idle effort and would

[9] But a supernatural curiosity to learn things about our heavenly home,
about the ways of its inhabitants and the secrets of their glory, about their
works and their thoughts, is laudable. The words, counsels and reflections
of Jesus, Mary and the Saints should be of intense and enthralling interest
for us.

[10] 1 Cor. xi. 1.

not promote a healthy spiritual life. We are to imitate the Saints in their endeavour to reproduce in their own lives the traits of the life of Jesus. He is the supreme Model of human conduct. He is most imitable. And each one of us is meant to reproduce according to his own personal endowments, his own mental and moral characteristics and his own individual measure of grace, his own personal expression of the human life of Jesus on earth. There can be as many imitations that are different, yet all true in their several measure, as there are individual Christians. Hence the following are the lines of imitation of the Saints that our conduct should pursue, if a profitable use is to be made of the reading of their lives.

(1) We should strive to conduct and ground our lives on the supernatural principles that guided theirs. In all their actions they were influenced only by supernatural values and did not allow themselves to be swayed by human motives. So too our conduct should not be determined by unchristian motives and principles, if we are to live a truly interior life.

(2) The Saints are meant to be an inspiration for us in the practice of those virtues which are the foundation of the christian life, in their whole-hearted service of God, in their complete subjection to His Will, in their contempt for the world, for its honours and advantages and in their spirit of self-sacrifice. Of course, the practice of these virtues must be adapted to the measure of our capacity. Thus, for instance, we must practise mortification after their model, but not necessarily in the form that the mortification took in their lives.

(3) We should admire the glory of God in the wonders He has accomplished in them ; they are the light of the world, they are those who have let their light shine before men that men might glorify their Father Who is in Heaven.

(4) Lastly, we should conceive a proper idea of the dignity and greatness of the Saints. Our lives are shaped subconsciously by our ideals. It is most important for us to have a true idea of real greatness and nobility of life. Amongst men the Saints alone are truly great in as much as they retrace in their life and conduct, the character of Him, who is undeniably, even for His enemies, the greatest amongst the sons of men. Beside His greatness, the greatness of those whom the world worships shows itself utterly false and shrunken. The Saints are the true heroes of humanity. They are the truly great men and great women because they closely resemble Him Who is the most perfect realisation of human greatness.

CHAPTER XVI

MORTIFICATION: A CONDITION OF LIFE

" Always bearing about in our body the mortification
of Jesus that the life also of Jesus may be made
manifest in our bodies." II Cor. iv. 10.

§1.   Disorder is in our soul from Adam's sin:
mortification aims at restoring order.

THE development of the supernatural virtues
in us is attended by a process which has a
twofold aspect. From one point of view this
process is one of decay and death, from another it is
one of expansion and life. The explanation lies in the
fact that a great disorder has been brought about in
our human nature by the fall, and this disorder even
though it has been repaired in its effects by the redeeming
grace of Our Saviour, has not been entirely healed;
the disarrangement in the powers of our nature has not
been undone except potentially. In other words, Our
Divine Lord has placed in our hands the means to repair
the disorder but has not destroyed it in its source.
One of the consequences of Adam's sin was the development in him of a vital activity hostile to the supernatural
life. This vital activity—which should be more accurately
characterised as devitalising activity—is the activity
of concupiscence. Everything that ministers energy
to this baneful activity, injures and tends to lower the
vital energy of the divine life of grace. In the language
of St. Paul, the evil and corrupting vitality is the life
of the flesh: that which it undermines and destroys

is the life of the spirit. Adam in revolting against God was punished by experiencing a general revolt throughout his whole being. Every faculty in his dual nature, that is, of sense and reason, asserting its independence, sought to develop its own vitality regardless of the general interest of the whole person, and made its own satisfaction the sole end of its activity. Self-gratification in its various forms became the object of life for man as swayed by the concupiscences— the sad heritage of original sin. The gratification sought after was not that which is proper to the personal, ordered activity of man, but that of each individual faculty capable of reaching after gratification. In the person of fallen man there reigned general anarchy.

Before the Fall, Adam's soul opened like a flower to the sun of Divine Influence. This Influence poured on his receptive spirit, flooded his intellect and will; it passed from the former faculty, that is, the intellect, into the imagination which held no image except such as had reference to God; from the other rational faculty, namely, the will, the divine influence passed into the senses which exercised themselves solely in obedience to the Divine Will faithfully transmitted to them by the human will which reflected the divine as a mirror. By the act of rebellion the stream from heaven was dried up at its source and the spiritual link which bound all the faculties was snapped. The result was that each faculty was, so to speak, left to its own devices with the consequence that was to be expected. Before the disaster there was only one term to the total activity of man and that was God—after the Fall there were as many ends to pursue as there were faculties to exercise themselves. Each blindly, obstinately pursued its own good. The will was dragged after every form of satisfaction. Owing to the greater vivacity of the apprehensive power of the senses and the weak appeal of the reason the satisfactions sought after were, for the most part, of a sensual kind. The reason which should and could preserve the whole man in order, had lost its certainty of vision after the initial error of breaking with God. Its dictates became uncertain and consequently its hold on the will became more feeble. The good it presented held out less attractions than that promised by the senses—hence the whole man tended to be dragged down the path of sensual self-gratification. Life became an effort to derive pleasure from every activity into which vital energy was poured. Error— giving as it does scope for self-indulgence—was forced on the will by the intelligence. Truth would exercise too much restraint over men's passions, hence it became an object of aversion for the appetitive rational faculty. Fallen man has a pronounced leaning towards what is false. The intellect following the way of the senses allowed itself to be carried away by precipitation and prejudice and swayed by an imagination that flattered ; it now sought as the term of its exercise not what was true, but what could please and especially what could justify the course of sensuality on which man had embarked. There is a marked tendency in fallen man to discover a philosophy which will justify his excesses and his aberrations. To justify his evil courses, he embraces error. "He would not understand that he might do well."[1] He shrinks from truth for it counsels

---

[1] " Noluit intelligere ut bene ageret." Ps, xxxv. 4.

restraint and right conduct. The triple concupiscence reigned supreme—the concupiscence of the flesh, that is, the thirst after sensible gratification in every form, the concupiscence of the eyes, that is, the pursuit of the pleasures that we have the power to conjure up for ourselves in imagination, and the pride of life, or the inordinate appetite for independence, for unchecked freedom of the will, and exaltation over one's fellows.

All the unregulated tendencies of men can be traced back to those three fountains. In whomsoever there is given free rein to those tendencies, " the charity of the Father is not in him ".[2] He lives the life of the world, the life that Christ reprobated, the life which checks his prayer at its source. The life according to the concupiscences is an existence which means spiritual death, and which tends even to its own decay, for the power of satisfying oneself decays with its own indulgence. The life of the concupiscences is a life which is a veritable dying, leading to a death that does not open to any life beyond. It is the spiritual form of that physical death which was inflicted on Adam for his sin ; for by it man as such tends to dwindle, in the darkening of his reason, in his growing subjection to perishable things, and in his abandonment of what is eternal and everlasting. The life according to the senses is death not only in the order of grace, but even in the order of nature. " For all that is in the world," says St. John, " is the concupiscence of the flesh, the concupiscence of the eyes and the pride of life, which is not of the Father, but is of the world."[3] The man governed by this triple concupiscence is the *old man*

---

[2] 1 St. John ii. 15.   [3] 1 St. John ii. 16.

of which St. Paul speaks, whose works are death, in contradistinction to the *new man*, that is, our nature as restored by Christ, with everything in that nature subject to God and filled with His life.

Mortification aims at the rectification of this disorder in our fallen nature, so that it may be replaced by that order in which sense is subject to reason and reason to God. By His Grace, Jesus Christ gave us power to recover, in a certain measure, this rectitude of our nature.[4] The function of mortification is to enable us to " strip ourselves of the old man with his deeds, and to put on the new, who is renewed unto knowledge, according to the image of him who created him ".[5] Mortification aims at replacing disorder by order, revolt against God and reason by subjection to Christ and His faith, disordered nature by vivifying grace, and self-indulgence by purity and justice. The ultimate effect is to reduce our senses to the control of our reason, our imagination to our will, and our will to God. It may be defined then as a deliberate renouncement of the life of disorderly satisfaction of our concupiscences, and a curbing of every inordinate exercise of our external and internal faculties. According to the signification of the word, it means a process of destruction, a dealing of death to that activity in us which seeks pleasure for the sake of pleasure ; its purpose

[4] The condition of restored human nature differs from the condition of nature in the state of original justice in this : In the state of original justice the subordination of sense to reason and reason to God could be maintained without any internal conflict. The maintenance of this right order in redeemed man even when his efforts are aided by grace, involves a severe struggle. The internal conflict remains even after original sin has been taken away. It is because of this that mortification is rigidly necessary. Without it then this internal conflict cannot issue in success for reason and faith.

[5] Coloss. iii. 9, 10.

is that this activity being deadened, the life received in baptism may have free scope for its development. It aims at death in order to secure life. If we are to realise our vocation as Christians this voluntary death is imposed on us : it is the condition of our sanctification. " Know ye not that all we who are baptised in Christ Jesus, are baptised in His death, for we are buried together with Him by Baptism unto death : that as Christ is risen from the dead by the glory of the Father, so we also may walk in newness of life."[6] Even as Christ " for the joy that was set before Him, endured the Cross ",[7] so we, by His Grace, endure the cross of mortification for the joy that gleams beyond the pathway of death, for the light towards which we stretch in the darkness, for the fulness of life in God towards which we are called and towards which by His Grace, we press forward. Mortification is an essential law of Christianity, a consequence of our incorporation with Christ. There is no possibility of receiving His life in our members, unless the activity of corrupt nature in those members is paralysed by self-inflicted privation. For mortification in its exercise involves the privation not only of unlawful satisfactions but even of those which in themselves are reasonable and legitimate.

§2.   The right use of Pleasure :
contentment of the mortified man.

It may seem a very rigorous law, that which imposes on us the necessity of denying ourselves even innocent gratifications. It seems scarcely possible to live without

[6] Rom. vi. 3, 4.   [7] Heb. xii. 2.

gratification of some kind or other. God, in fashioning our nature, has indeed united a sense of satisfaction with the normal and healthy exercise of each one of our faculties. Any activity that is exercised with facility and on some object which is not beyond the capacity of our powers is accompanied by a feeling of keen delight. This is true for the exercise of reason as well as for the play of the senses. The intelligent and keen-witted find great happiness in grappling with problems which, whilst testing their powers to the utmost, still hold out a possibility of solution. The painter and the sculptor experience great joy in the sense of power they have in using the materials of their arts to express the beautiful concepts of their minds. The musician finds a charm in calling forth and grouping harmonious sounds : the nature lover feels a deep contentment when the eye rests upon a scene all the beauty of which it is able to appreciate. The intellectual find pleasure in the exercise of the mind, and the strong limbed in testing the powers of the body. Finding this pleasure that accompanies the normal play of our faculties appetising, we have a tendency to seek that form of activity to which we feel our powers proportionate, and to shun all that seems to present great difficulty or to be beyond our capacity. We are tempted to pursue not what we ought, but what holds out promise of pleasure. Disorder begins when seeking only *mere gratification* we renounce everthing which does not promise it, and make everything we do minister it to us. We are meant by God to make use of delectation, to make it serve our purposes, to find in it an aid to surmounting the tediousness of life ; we misuse it when we make it an end, not a means.

All immortification may be reduced to this—the pursuit of satisfaction of mind or body as an end. Our Lord's life was the very antithesis of this. As St. Paul says : " Christ did not please Himself ".[8] He did not seek His own satisfaction in what He did. He acted not under the stimulus of pleasure but of Divine charity.

Were our nature not so corrupted by sin, it would be sufficient for us to practise temperance and use pleasure in moderation. But so strong is the attraction which pleasure exercises over us, so powerful is its appeal, such a response does it find in us to its allurements, that the taste of it is dangerous for us. It is difficult to yield to its influence without running the risk of exceeding in the measure of it we accord to ourselves. To school ourselves to the right use of delectation, we must begin by starving our craving for it : we must be more than temperate in its regard, we must be mortified—insensible, as it were, and dead to its call.[9] In the restraint we have to exercise over the senses, over the imagination and over the will, Religion demands more of us than reason. It is not sufficient to prescribe the limits of reason to the bodily appetites, we must, in order to make the body obedient to reason and faith, chastise it and reduce it to subjection[10] by depriving it of many gratifications legitimate enough in themselves and in the abstract. The more that is conceded to the body the less it is satisfied and the greater are its demands. The body will not be a good servant until it has been consistently deprived of what it has strictly a right to. Our Lord has set us the example for this rigorous

[8] Rom. xv. 3.
[9] Cf. *Exercises of St. Ignatius*, Additions x.
[10] 1 Cor. ix. 27.

treatment of ourselves. We shall not have order and
peace in our powers, contentment in our mind, and
docility to the inspiration of grace in our soul, unless
we reduce to practice the lesson given us by Him.
This involves the patient, constant and unremitting
mortification of all our tendencies—resolutely denying
ourselves in many things—"always," as St. Paul
advises us, "bearing about in our body the mortification
of Jesus, that the life also of Jesus may be made manifest
in our bodies".[11]

This is to face, apparently, a very sombre and dreary
existence—one which seems but a dull and grey vista
of years stretching as far as the tomb and unrelieved
by any ray of colour or brightness. This is not
so. Far from making for sadness, self-abnegation
brings us a joy which self-indulgence never can.
Self-indulgence promises happiness, but provides
nothing but restlessness and discontent and disillusionment. On the other hand, self-denial even as
inspired by religion holds out no prospect of gratification and yet it begets the greatest joy that this life
can discover—the contentment which comes from
the tranquillity of order in ourselves. It brings the
untroubled conscience and the cessation of all restless
and gnawing cravings; it ministers that "peace of God,
which surpasseth all understanding". But to secure
this effect, our mortification must be thorough; it
must affect our interior as well as our exterior, our
minds as well as our senses. To confine ourselves to
bodily penance and to neglect the curbing of our interior
powers is to perform a useless task; whilst on the

[11] 2 Cor. iv. 10.

other hand to neglect corporal mortifications in the pretence of devoting oneself to interior ones as being of much more importance, is to engage ourselves in a futile endeavour. To combat the triple concupiscence which nurtures the life of "the old man" in us, and stifles the life of the new, we must mortify our senses, our imagination and our reason, and we must encourage ourselves to do so by the thought that it is utterly impossible to lead a truly interior and spiritual life without the continual mortification of ourselves under this triple aspect. With the gift of Faith, every Christian receives the light to understand, at least to a certain extent, that mortification must form an integral part of his life as a follower of Christ. It costs, of course, to keep free from mortal sin, and to resist the temptations that incline us to it. There is penance in this, but each one has the conviction that the life of mortification, which aims at nothing higher than the curbing of the satisfactions that involve mortal sin, will fail of its purpose; the christian sense warns a man that unless his rebellious nature receives harsher treatment than is involved in the checking of its sinful inclinations, he will in the end yield to the seduction of evil. The Christian feels instinctively that he must mortify himself. It is a hard necessity, an unpleasant occupation, but it obtrudes itself insistently on the christian conscience. Its demands cannot be evaded. But corrupt nature even when yielding to necessity will seek compensation for what it surrenders. It happens frequently that we mortify ourselves readily on some one point or other and so satisfy our conscience that we are conforming ourselves to the law of Christianity. Having given a salve to our conscience by exercising restraint in one direction we give a free rein to self-indulgence in another : we curb our desire to speak, for instance, and give free play to curiosity, by putting no check to our desires of seeing : we may be exact in our observance of the law of fasting, and very lax in the observation of the law of charity : and it is possible to find Christians who chastise themselves with the discipline and chastise others with their tongues. Holy Scripture speaks very ironically of this partial exercise of penance. "Behold in the day of your fast your own will is found, and you exact of all your debtors. Is this such a fast as I have chosen for a man to afflict his soul for a day ? Is this it, to wind his head about like a circle, and to spread sackcloth and ashes, wilt thou call this a fast and a day acceptable to the Lord ? Is not this rather the fast I have chosen ? Loose the bonds of wickedness, undo the bundles that oppress, let them that are broken go free, and break asunder every burden. Deal thy bread to the hungry, and bring the needy and harbourless into thy house : then shall thy light break forth as the morning, and thy health shall speedily arise, and thy justice shall go before thy face, and the glory of the Lord shall gather thee up."[12]

§3.   The Practice of Mortification

In the work of gaining control of our disorderly appetites by mortification, the beginner must keep well in mind the facility in prayer, the happiness and the intimacy with God which will be the consequence of

[12] Isaias lviii. 3–8.

a life of generous and persevering mortification. He should begin with limited but fixed points on which mortification will be practised. By degrees things will become easier and his mortification will be extended without extraordinary difficulty. In the account we propose to give of the practice of mortification, we set before the reader a picture of the perfectly mortified man. We show the goal to be aimed at rather than the first practice to be put before the beginner.

Mortification should begin with the senses, and when these are taught restraint, not much difficulty will be experienced in controlling the interior. For by the denial of their gratifications to the external faculties, the imagination itself is starved of all that can excite in it pleasant, agreeable and sensual images. The intellect depends for its exercise to a large extent on the imagination, and the will in its turn is attracted only by what the intellect presents to it as good and as worthy of being sought; hence when that faculty, namely the imagination, which stores the impressions conveyed by the senses, is rectified in its activity, the operation of the higher or spiritual faculties will in their turn be in order. This is generally true but, still, the rule may admit of exceptions. There are persons who are faultless as far as this life of the senses is concerned, and yet offend God mortally by an intolerable pride. The malice of sin of this kind, the deliberate pursuit of the satisfaction arising from the sense of one's own excellence, is diabolic in character and more grievous in the sight of God than any disorder of the flesh. The work of mortification consists in frustrating the work of sin everywhere, arresting its development, and stamping out the seeds of it that are found in the soul even when it has been regenerated in baptism. Mortification deals its assaults on a dual objective. It exercises itself on the outward and on the inward man, and accordingly is either interior or exterior. To mortify oneself merely under one to the exclusion of the other of those two aspects is practically to lose one's time. Without the double mortification, what St. Paul called the " Flesh " is not sufficiently subdued.

Our sensitive faculties first must be submitted to a regular treatment, consisting in a consistent thwarting of their desires. It is not a question of depriving ourselves of the use of our senses but of securing that use of them which shall be in accord with the demands of our rational as well as of our supernatural being—the demands of reason and faith. To secure this we must regularly, at least in the beginning, refuse them what might legitimately be accorded them. We ought to submit them not only to restraint and privation, but to positive suffering in order to be sure to secure order in their activities. The following paragraphs describe the rule of conduct to be followed in order to bring the senses perfectly under control. The advices there given are in the abstract clear enough, and a knowledge of them is essential, but in their application to each soul imprudences are possible. Hence in this question of the mortification of the senses, it is well for us to submit our course of action to a prudent spiritual guide. We shall thus be protected from the natural error of being too lenient on ourselves and so effecting nothing ; what is more important we shall be saved from that excess in this matter which is the pitfall of so many beginners. The soul on the threshold of the spiritual life all impatient to eradicate from itself defects only too apparent, is prone, unless guided by a skilled director, to adopt a course of action impossible because it is beyond its actual forces at the moment or beyond the movements of grace. Only too soon it will abandon its attempt as hopeless, and in all likelihood will cease altogether from practices of mortification to its great spiritual detriment.

We should mortify our eyes not lending them to the gratification of an idle curiosity. Not only should we not rest them on objects the sight of which in themselves constitutes sin, but we should withhold them from regarding any creature the contemplation of which might excite undue disturbances in our imagination. We should not look merely to derive satisfaction from our regards without any ultimate justification. That is the negative side of the obligation. Taking the matter positively what we allow ourselves to see should give us either the reasonable recreation that our body needs, or serve to provide for the elevation of our mind. As we grow in the spiritual life we should use our faculty of vision to contemplate the divine beauty in creatures and thereby to raise our souls to God.

We should mortify our sense of hearing by training ourselves to shut our ears to what merely pleases or flatters us. We should curb our desire to hear, when we expect that what we are to listen to will provide food for our vanity or our self-love. We should not be anxious to hear what is favourable to ourselves, nor should we be ready to give ear to what is unfavourable to others. Under pain of sin we must not allow ourselves to listen to bad or uncharitable conversations : under risk of having the purity of our conscience tarnished we must be rigorous in curbing our curiosity to hear things, the knowledge of which we had better be without. To seek for news is merely to open a wide gate to a multitude of distractions. Those who cultivate an interior life should desire to hear only what might furnish food for noble thought or increase their knowledge of God. They should be eager to be told not of the things of this world but of the things of the next. Not that we should at all times have our minds tense : good sense and understanding will dictate that at times it is useful and may be obligatory to take part in conversations that have as their object to refresh, to amuse and to recreate. Furthermore, we can practise a good deal of mortification by being good listeners, especially when the speaker happens to be a dull or tedious or uninteresting talker. Charity will order us at times of recreation not to seek conversations that are agreeable, and not to fly from those that are otherwise. Interior souls should deliberately refuse themselves the gratification of conversations that bring with them the spirit of the world—and should not allow themselves when they are obliged to entertain, to be dragged into talk which would make subsequent contact with God difficult. They should lift up others, rather than be pulled down themselves. Musicians should exercise a check on their desire to hear music, should deliberately shut their ears to all that is merely sensuous, and should refuse themselves the pleasure of hearing again in their imagination the good music that appeals to them.

We must mortify our sense of taste. Fasting should hold a place in our lives, and we should be far from seeking reasons to escape its obligations. It promotes the well-being of the body as well as that of the soul; and with the mitigations that have been introduced into it, there is little fear of its doing any injury to the health.[13] Fasting is to be done at certain times, but abstinence should be the ordinary condition of our lives. Besides the ordinary weekly abstinence which we should accept as a mortification imposed by the Church for our benefit, it is good to season each meal with some little penance or other. The mortified Christian is sparing in the use of condiments, and takes what is good for him rather than that which merely pleases the palate. It is useful occasionally to forego the use of condiments altogether—though this must not be done often. As a general rule, St. Francis de Sales observes it is better to take what is going or what comes our way rather than to choose what is worst and he is but explaining the words of Christ: " Eat what is set before you ". Eating outside of mealtimes is best avoided; and to take food simply because we happen to feel hungry, or to drink simply because we happen to feel thirsty, is a sign of great immortification. It is not too much to ask a follower of Christ to endure the pangs of hunger and thirst until the time for refection comes around.

The sense of touch is the most dangerous of all the senses and demands an exercise of the most rigorous mortification. This sense furnishes the sharpest tempta-

[13]However, even in the case of fasting, it is well to consult our confessor or director, especially if there be question of a fast not imposed by the Church or by rule, and we should humbly accept his decision.

tions and provides at the same time the most numerous
occasions for chastising the body. Christian modesty
and decorum demand a great reserve in the use of the
hands. We should forbid ourselves any touch that
has no other end but to yield a sensible gratification—
even though that gratification may not be sinful. To
secure a mastery over our bodies it is necessary to
discipline them carefully in this matter; we should
aim at eliminating all undue seeking of comfortable
or easy positions, and an attitude indicative of indolence
or surrender to self-indulgence should be carefully
avoided. In sitting, standing or walking, great care
should be taken to hold the body well: the cultivation
of a proper ' tenue ' carries with it a great deal of corporal
penance which has the double advantage of procuring
a mastery over the body, and imparting that dignity
which becomes a Christian whose body is the Tabernacle
of the Holy Ghost. In our occupations, in our recreations
and at our prayers, constant efforts must be made to
hold the body well. We may take a restful position
but never a nonchalant one. The sense of touch may
also be mortified excellently by submitting uncom-
plainingly to the inclemencies of the weather, and by
the patient and reasonable endurance of the discomforts
of both heat and cold. This regular discipline of ourselves will ensure that we be able to accomplish that most
difficult of all things, namely, to bear sickness well and
to make it profitable to our souls; and at the same time
it will enable us to banish from our minds an excessive
concern for our health.[14]   Even religious persons are

[14]This usually expresses itself in a tendency to complain of little ailments.
Of these St. Teresa says, " if you can endure them say nothing about them ";
and she adds, " if you cause self-love to die, you will experience mortification

found who make a fetish of it: "They seem," says St. Teresa, "to have entered religion for no other purpose than to secure that the date of their death be postponed to the utmost limit possible ". In a word, we must not aim at weakening our body, but at making it a useful servant to our souls. We should not deprive it of what it needs, but we should refuse it what is superfluous.

Our next efforts should be directed against the imagination. Once the senses are mortified, this task of mortification of the imagination has much of the difficulty removed. On the contrary supposition it is impossible. The imagination can procure us great delectation by picturing vividly to us the pleasures to come, and by conjuring up visions of those that have been enjoyed already. We must not seek to taste what is in anticipation nor savour what is past. It is a defect to use our imagination for calling up pleasant sights or scenes or associations especially those that flatter self-love or sensuality: its employ should be solely for the purpose of subserving useful or good processes of thought. To lend it to reverie or day-dreaming is to embark on a course which will eventually end in temptation and very likely in sin.

If we exclude from our imagination images that merely procure pleasure and preserve only those that can serve our intellectual and our spiritual life, the control of the reason will be easy. It too requires its own dis-

---

in all the attention and care bestowed on you, you will only accept the same from necessity ". Nevertheless our endurance of heat or cold must not be pushed too far, it must not be such as would *in a short time* cause serious injury to health. Here again the advice of a director will ensure that the limits of prudence are not transgressed.

cipline. Work and pursuit of true knowledge with a view to knowing God and His world better and so serving Him in a more enlightened manner, provides the exercise which will maintain the intellect in order. The pursuit of knowledge is arduous and carries with it a severe penance. All are tempted to intellectual indolence, and it is more criminal to yield to it than to bodily sloth for it carries with it more serious consequences. We should use our minds to do our work efficiently in the service of God, not for the satisfaction that we may find in intellectual exercise. For the intellect as it develops power finds an intense satisfaction in a study which in its beginning was irksome. There is danger here that we shall be tempted to give our time to that form of mental work in which we find satisfaction to the neglect of that which is distasteful, even when duty imposes the latter. Method in our work, a limited time given to the studies that satisfy, and a sufficient time given to those that are necessary or useful will finally give us a keen, disciplined, controlled and mortified intelligence.

Being exercised in what is right, our intellect will have nothing but objects that have the form of truth or beauty or utility to present to the will and the movement of the latter will always be in the direction of what is right and reasonable. The will submitted to grace and reason is the will that is submitted to God. This submission of the will to the divine impulse and the renouncement of the following of its own caprices, constitutes its mortification.[15] Thus there is created

[15]This mortification of the will is nothing else than the mortification of our desires. St. John of the Cross, in the *Ascent of Mount Carmel*, points out the supreme importance of this mortification: he shows how desires

order in the whole man and the efforts of the triple concupiscence are destroyed : the senses and the imagination are brought under the government of the reason, the reason is controlled by the will, and the latter faculty moves obediently to the order of the Divine Will. Thus is perfect charity acquired, the way prepared for the closest and most intimate union and the whole person thoroughly mortified without appearing, even to that person's most intimate acquaintances, in the least out of the ordinary. The mortification described is perfect and effective and yet preserves him who practises it from the danger of the pride that follows indulgence in penances that are singular or extraordinary. It often causes surprise to souls filled with generosity and goodwill to discover a discrepancy between the directions they receive from their spiritual advisers and the injunctions laid down in spiritual books. The latter insist on the necessity of the practice of bodily mortifications, whereas the spiritual guides habitually manifest a reluctance to give any concessions on this point when permission is sought for the use of corporal austerities. The difference between theory and practice is but apparent. There is a real danger that the unskilled in the ways of the soul may make *use of mortifications* to *evade mortification*. When nature is chastised in one direction, its tendency is to seek an outlet in another. Particular bodily mortifications may easily give the soul the persuasion that it is mortified, and lull it into

---

torment and darken and pollute the soul and he declares that by mortification of our desires we would make greater progress in a month than we could make in many years by imprudent methods of devotion. And he adds: " neither can the darkness and ignorance of our souls be removed if desires are not quenched ". (Bk. I, ch. 8.)

a sense of security as regards the rest of its conduct and actions. Mortified on one point the soul may allow itself to be unmortified on many others. This is a real danger against which the spiritual guide must be on his guard. A general and universal curb on this tendency to self-gratification for gratification's sake, is better than acts of penance confined to one particular matter. Still, this danger of the misuse of corporal austerities should not discourage their use. Even though beginners make mistakes in the exercise of bodily penances these mistakes are corrected by time and goodwill with prudent directions. The awkward movements of the child must precede the assured and firm step of the adult. Corporal mortifications are to be commended in spite of the risks that attend their use.

Well-ordered, thorough and persevering discipline of the higher and lower powers of the soul, coupled with wisely directed bodily austerities fulfils the injunction of always bearing about in our body the mortification of Christ. By reason of it the whole man gradually comes into order, the disarrangement wrought by sin diminishes, and God's action proceeds apace in the soul—" the life of Jesus is made manifest in our bodies ". The removal of the obstacles to grace is then the aim of mortification as it is also the aim of prayer. But it is attained by neither of them alone ; both work hand in hand. Prayer soon ceases, if unaided by mortification ; mortification can spring only from pride and end only in dissatisfaction when it is not originated and sustained by a prayerful spirit. The labour, pain and anguish experienced by the soul that enters on the hard way of prayer and mortification seem very uninviting, and so they are, but the sweet peace and unspeakable contentment, well known to those who have persevered, so far outweigh initial suffering as to make it appear negligible. This must needs be, for of what importance is any temporal distress when viewed in conjunction with the attainment of that end for which we were created, the all-sufficing possession of God reigning within the soul as in His temple and sharing with it His own happiness.

CHAPTER XVII

SILENCE: A MEANS TO RECOLLECTION

" In silence and quiet the devout soul goeth forward and learneth the secrets of the Scripture." Imit. 1. 20. 6.

§1.   The Decline in Spiritual Life.

THE most painful experience in the spiritual life is that of the vicissitudes to which it is subject. At times all goes well with us; borne along by the strong current of grace, all the obstacles of nature and temperament yield before us. Acts of virtue are accomplished without difficulty and even joyously; prayer is of astonishing ease; sacrifice is a pleasure, and the service of God a service of deep happiness. The soul is filled with buoyancy and with a joyous eager anticipation, for sanctity and the unbroken union with God which is its result, seem within easy reach. And suddenly, for no apparent reason, something as it were snaps; devotion and the fine sense of the supernatural disappear, and we are left in the hard biting chilling atmosphere of unregenerate nature; faults and imperfections multiply, the exercise of virtue becomes extremely arduous, and the yielding to our own temperament, with all the laxity and absence of spirituality that belongs to this surrender, seems inevitable. The fair form of sanctity which spurred us on to effort and which we thought we were on the point of embracing, eludes our grasp and fades like a mirage of the desert; we thought that we were quite close to God, and we find that He is as far off from us as ever. The pain of keen disappointment attends the experience. The soul, ignorant of itself, while attributing this failure either to an intrinsic impossibility in the realisation of the ideal it had set before it, or at least to an incompatibility between that ideal and itself, will be tempted to renounce the enterprise it has engaged on as hopeless, and its object as unattainable.

For souls that are of a heroic mould and that are somewhat advanced in the ways of God, this sub-traction of fervour and the insipidity that is found in spiritual things after the withdrawal, is a trial that serves for the increase of their merits and for their greater perfection. But for ordinary souls it is to be traced back to the infidelities into which they have allowed themselves to drift—at least in most cases. The divine life in us is of extreme delicacy, because it is a participation of the life of God Himself—a very little thing can affect its vigour and diminish its glow: " we have this treasure in earthen vessels ".[1] It can be easily struck at by forces hostile to it and when not actually destroyed, have its vitality diminished. The least breath of nature (i.e. egoism) can weaken it. It cannot retain its strength and perfection except every deliberate and conscious activity of the soul is under the inspiration of grace. When, owing to carelessness or want of spiritual discernment, or both combined, the soul allows itself to follow the promptings of nature or of temperament, the life of charity instantly loses its fervour, and there is a lowering of supernatural vitality ; this lowering of vitality carries with it an inability to

[1] 2 Cor. iv. 7.

elicit readily and promptly or at least a great difficulty in eliciting readily and promptly acts of the supernatural life. This diminution of purely supernatural activity is intensified by the decrease in the number of actual graces accorded the soul, by reason of its infidelities, rendering itself unworthy to receive them. Every supernatural vital movement that the soul, in the exercise of the divine life in it, tends to elicit, appeals for—and that by the very nature of things—the actual grace that is required in order that the act produced may be worthy of and commensurate with the principle of life from which it issues. That is, the soul striving to act supernaturally needs and receives the actual grace needed to carry this striving into effect. On the other hand if the soul stirs into movement under the impulse of nature, its act has not any exigency of supernatural help, and ordinarily, in consequence, this is not accorded. When such a condition of things becomes habitual, it is evident that much of the activity of the soul issues forth at the prompting of nature, and uninfluenced by grace. It is not then astonishing that acts inspired and motived by charity become rare and difficult.

There is nothing which so quickly causes this decline in fervour as the failure to maintain proper reserve in the use of the tongue. It is surprising, but nevertheless true, that we more easily fail in speech than in any other form of doing. There is comparatively little difficulty in focusing plenty of attention on the action we accomplish either in obedience to rule or at the call of duty; but to carry on a conversation and maintain oneself in one's words in a spirit of faith for a considerable length of time is within the power of comparatively few. Only those who have attained to a certain measure of sanctity succeed in this. If there is in us any passion, which has not been perfectly subdued, that passion will, very frequently, in any conversation that is somewhat prolonged, begin to exercise its influence on thoughts and judgments and speech and betray us into the fault to which that passion inclines us.

Control of the tongue might seem only one element in the ascetic discipline that the pursuit of perfection demands. One might easily imagine that after the use of speech has been brought under the control of reason and faith there would remain much to accomplish. This is not so, for it is hardly possible that perfectly regulated speech exists until all the senses are brought well under control. This is the truth conveyed in St. James' words : " If any man offend not in word, that same is a perfect man ". He had just said, " For in many things we all offend ".[2] The sequence of thought implies, therefore, that if a man does not offend in words, he has reached a point of perfection when he offends in nothing, that is to say that he is in the habitual exercise of all the virtues. There is profound psychological insight in this, as will be shown later.

§2.   Silence one of the Church's Traditional
Antidotes to Spiritual Decline.

The practice of silence has been recognised from all times as the sole means of arriving at this government of the tongue, without which saintliness of life is

[2] St. James iii. 2.

impossible. The Apostle insists that " if any man think himself to be religious, not bridling his tongue, but deceiving his own heart, this man's religion is vain ".[3] The early solitaries fled from the intercourse of men and even from intercourse with one another, depriving themselves for long years of the use of the faculty of speech, so alive were they to the havoc caused to the interior life by the immoderation into which the use of the tongue so often degenerates. And even when they began to group themselves together in Monasteries, the solitude of their lives was scarcely interfered with. They restricted their intercourse to what was barely necessary. In this they felt they were following in the footsteps of Our Divine Lord Himself Who, for our example and instruction, showed such a marked preference for silence and retirement, and a habitual restraint in the use of words. In the Holy House of Nazareth, the spoken words must have been but few. Our Lord's time had not come for manifesting Himself. His Parents had to use their supernatural discernment to grasp the significance of His hidden Life. He vouchsafed no information. Mary and Joseph spoke little but pondered much in the depths of their souls on the mystery which daily developed before their eyes. Words would have been an intrusion and would have but disturbed the course of thought, which in each, under the illumination of the Holy Ghost, discovered new and profounder meanings in the prophecies which they knew so well and the realisation of which they saw taking place under their own roof.

This life of silence, broken only by words that come

[3] St. James i. 26.

from souls occupied habitually with the thought of God, was the ideal that the Founders of the great Contemplative Orders had before them as they framed the rules of their Institutes. They realised clearly that perfection could not be practised in their monasteries unless the intercourse of the religious with one another, or with strangers, should be reduced to what should be demanded by necessity or Charity. Conversation was strictly forbidden during the hours of work and of prayer—it was forbidden at all times except at recreation. And even then it was enjoined that the subjects treated of should be such as could prove of general interest, should tend to elevate whilst recreating the mind and should also impart edification.

In order that this calm tranquillity of the houses should be at all times undisturbed, talking was prohibited not only in the oratories but in almost all parts of the interior of the religious houses. It was understood that conversation in the corridors, cells or refectories, even during the hours of recreation, would banish the atmosphere of undisturbed quiet, which, as was recognised, it was necessary to maintain in all those places where souls were encouraged to commune with God. Silence consecrated not only the hours of work and prayer, but even the very quarters which the religious habitually frequented. And when the day's task drew to a close this silence deepened and became more impenetrable—nothing but matters of the greatest necessity was allowed to break in upon the stillness that descended on the monastery and wrapped it round, as it were, in a thick mantle, from the end of Vespers until the conclusion of the Mass and Office of the following morning. All modern religious societies have followed the earlier ones in this respect; the time from night prayers until the termination of the Morning Office is called in all Institutes, the time of " great silence ". When the rule in this matter of silence is well observed fervour flourishes and the peace of God reigns. It has been said with truth that all that is needed to reform a house that has fallen into lukewarmness, is that the rule of silence begin to be perfectly observed. The same is true of the individual soul that is eager for its advancement in the spiritual life; if it pays strict attention to due restraint of speech flagging devotion will revive.

§3.   The Power of the Tongue for Good or Evil.

There appears something paradoxical in this attitude of the Masters of perfection towards the exercise of the faculty of speech. They seem to judge that the best use of the tongue is to use it as little as possible. Yet speech is our noblest prerogative; it exalts us above the animals. The tongue serves to manifest the thoughts of our minds and the determinations of our wills. The faculty of articulate utterance has been given us by God Himself to sound His praises, to proclaim His glory and to establish useful and friendly intercourse with one another. It can procure immense good in the natural as well as in the supernatural order. Who can measure the good effects of a kind word, or set limits to its power to bring consolation to weary spirit or wounded heart? It is the words of wisdom that fell from Our Divine Lord's lips that have reformed the world. What would the world be like if He had not spoken? And had not these words been lovingly treasured by His followers, and found fresh utterance on their lips, His message would not have reached the ears of mankind—would not have passed beyond the narrow confines of His own land. It is to their bold speech that we owe the priceless gift of Faith. " Faith cometh by hearing ; and hearing by the word of Christ. But I say; have they not heard? Yes, verily; their sound hath gone forth unto all the earth: and their words unto the ends of the whole world."[4] It is by words pronounced by human lips that the substance of bread is changed into the Body of Our Lord, and Jesus is made present with us. The priest speaks and as his voice dies away, the tide of absolution flows on the sinner's soul, washing away the darkest stains; and when God's minister pronounces the formula of Baptism, the slave of Satan is elevated from his servile state to the exalted condition of a child of God. And day by day the whole earth resounds with the praises of its Creator, as from countless choirs ascend to heaven in human accents the inspired utterances of the Holy Spirit. The great work of the Church is the Divine Office, and it needs human lips and human voices for its accomplishment. It would seem strange then, seeing that speech is the source of so much good in the natural and supernatural order, that the discipline of perfection should apparently demand its suppression.

There is no contradiction involved; for silence is not the cult of dumbness nor of a morose taciturnity. It is a discipline undertaken in order to use the faculty

[4] Rom. x. 17, 18.

of speech in such a way as shall profit and not prove
harmful to the soul. It is only by silence that the use
of the tongue is brought into order and made to subserve
the purpose for which it was given to us by God. This
purpose was twofold. We are given articulate speech
to speak the praises of God and to promote His glory—
according to the words of St. Paul: " Be ye filled with
the Holy Spirit, speaking to yourselves in psalms and
hymns and spiritual canticles, singing and making
melody in your hearts to the Lord ; giving thanks always
for all things, in the name of Our Lord Jesus Christ,
to God and the Father ".[5] The other purpose aimed
at by God in this gift of speech was that it should be
a means of promoting harmonious, recreative, friendly,
charitable and informative intercourse between men
living in social relations with one another.

The tongue like the other sensible faculties needs
to pass through a rigid mortification before its exercise
can be made subject to reason. And as the tongue is
more difficult to control its discipline must be harder
and more stern than that which is needed for the other
faculties. " The tongue is a fire," says St. James, " a
world of iniquity."[6] And where there is much talk,
sin will not be wanting, as we are told in the Book
of Proverbs.[7] How few there are who have not
experienced at some time or other how a single
conversation can cause to disappear the good effects
wrought in the soul by a fervent meditation ! To
understand how this is so it is necessary to study the
motives that prompt us to speak. If we exclude the
circumstances in which the amenities of social life compel

---

[5] Eph. v. 18-20.   [6] St. James iii. 6.   [7] Prov. x. 19.

us to draw on our minds or memories in order to contribute our share to making the time pass agreeably and in an interesting manner, if we leave out of count the occasions when necessity or duty oblige us to speak to those with whom we have to deal, we shall find that almost invariably it is a motive springing from the egoism of our unregenerate nature that prompts us to utterance.

It is true that Man is by nature communicative and not solitary. Nothing belongs so intimately to nature, says Maximus,[8] as to share the thoughts of our mind one with another, and God has attached to the exercise of the power of communicating our thoughts a satisfaction which we should consider as the gift of His kindness. In this, as in the exercise of the other human faculties, there is a temptation to subordinate the use to the enjoyment. There is in fallen man a tendency to seek satisfaction for satisfaction's sake. This tendency is very pronounced in the case of the use of the tongue. The habitual talker, the man who has not been disciplined by silence, tends to talk for the mere gratification he finds therein irrespective of any good or legitimate end to be achieved thereby. There can be a disordered self-satisfaction in imparting information when not utility or charity but one's own egoism is served by the giving of the information. The unmortified seek this gratification with avidity. The " exteriorised " soul—the extroverted—to use a term used by early English mystical writers, is ever eager to impart news. He desires to experience the sense of superiority that springs from the consciousness of the possession of knowledge not held by those to whom he is making

[8] *Catena Aurea*, in Luc. Evan. x.

his communication. The uncontrolled person is easily tempted to break through rule or cast aside restraint in order to taste this pleasure which is purely egoistical. And if, as may happen, though rarely, communicativeness is inspired by a desire to confer a benefit on another, even in this case it may be, in part at least, vitiated by a satisfaction administered to our inordinate desire of superiority.

It is not only sensible satisfaction that is sought in the exercise of the faculty of speech. Pride, very frequently, is at the root of the inordinate use of the tongue. It is a great power to be able to call ideas into being in the mind of another. The listener becomes in a certain sense the subject of him by whose speech his mind is gripped and set in activity in a new direction. The influence exercised by the gift of persuasive words is real and lasting. There is in each one of us the ardour of the propagandist—even concerning indifferent things. It is pride more often than the zeal for truth, that urges us to bring those with whom we converse to see things as we see them. Impatient of opposition and eager to persuade, we try to monopolise the conversation, and find difficulty in confining our remarks to the times that call for speech. We are hurried by our unmortified eagerness to leave aside restraint, and to pour out arguments, as soon as they form themselves in our imagination, into the ears of those we desire to persuade. It is almost invariably want of restraint over natural impetuosity, absence of control of the imagination, and a craving to satisfy our egoistic tendencies in one way or another that prompts immediate and useless speaking. Seeing then that speech occurs at the very moment that purely natural and, at the best, imperfect tendencies are seeking satisfaction, and since the stirring into activity of these tendencies is the occasion of speech, it is only of rigid consequence that men in their words should be betrayed into numberless faults.

There is a close and intimate connection between speech and the imagination. Idle and vain words call up idle and vain images in the imagination.[9] These images summon others of a kindred sort, in virtue of what is called the law of the association of ideas. In this way a train of flattering, useless and egoistic images is started. Thought follows imagination and participates in its self-gratifying tendencies. Speech follows thoughts and words flow that do not bear on subjects that have a tendency to supernaturalise the soul either of speaker or listener. In conversation words are interchanged and multiplied; corresponding images are called up; and thought follows all the time the direction set by the vocal and mental images. Hence in profane conversation our mind is caught up and carried along in the stream of natural activity, which becomes more and more contaminated the further it is removed from the source; for in its course it is ever gathering up material of a more and more dubious nature.

When the conversations are very intimate and take place between those drawn together by some natural sympathy, the evil is intensified. An egoism of a far worse nature than mere vanity, or sense of gratification,

[9] " Every idle word men shall speak, they shall render an account of it in the day of judgment. " St. Matt. xii. 36.

or the desire to excel, or the eagerness to exercise power, comes into play when not charity or justice but mere selfish liking draws people together in intercourse : in this case the conversation will almost invariably take a certain wrong direction. Things that will be said will proceed from the desire to give free play to the expression of one's sympathies or one's antipathies— and more frequently the latter than the former. All the passions of our sensitive nature are rooted in and spring from our loves or our hates—or perhaps our likings or our dislikings if we are incapable of such strong emotions as love or hate. If we are not accustomed to control both likes and dislikes ; if we are wont to have our actions swayed and determined by these emotions ; if we are not mortified enough to oppose constantly our inordinate inclinations ; if we make no effort to meet on friendly terms those we dislike or to avoid the company of those to whom we have a leaning, it is impossible that our words will remain for any length of time on an indifferent or an elevated topic. Uncharitableness and murmuring will presently make their appearance.

Our words and the words of those who share our views will fan to intensity the passions which perhaps in the beginning of the conversations were not very active ; our likes and dislikes will become sharpened and with this will be awakened all the other evil passions which are rooted in our sympathies and antipathies, namely, jealousy, anger, envy and the rest. So that in one conversation it will become possible to commit faults against a large number of virtues. " And the tongue," says St. James, " is a fire and inflameth the wheel of our nativity, being set on fire by hell."[10] This is perfectly accurate, for when our words are set going by the stimulus of a base motive, each passion, one after the other, is set alight in the course of the conversation. One can imagine a series of lamps each springing into flame in its turn at the application of the devil's torch. The uncontrolled use of the tongue or a use dictated by egoism will drag us into sins against charity, justice, truthfulness, forbearance, reverence, kindness, etc. And it is possible for a single conversation, taking its rise in a movement of nature, to issue in faults of all these various kinds—not only is it possible but, if the talk is prolonged enough, it almost invariably happens.

§4. How to Control the Tongue.

To keep in check, then, the passions, which in their activity destroy the bonds of union, uproot charity and make common life unbearable, it is necessary to exercise a rigid control over the tongue. In the beginning, to acquire this control we must cut down our words more than will be found necessary in a later stage of development. Silence must be kept with scrupulous exactitude. Occasionally such a rigid adherence to silence may seem insincere. When we feel a tumult within us with all the passions raging and clamouring for expression it will seem that we are so wicked that it would be just as well to speak out our mind. It seems that when we feel so bad there is nothing to be gained by not expressing our badness. This is a mistake. If a person for a continuous period strongly checks every

[10] St. James iii. 6.

impulse to express his emotions, these emotions gradually
lose their force and vivacity. Every passion, somehow,
becomes unnerved when it cannot express itself.
Expression seems to be the fuel that sustains it ; deprived
of this fuel it dies down like a fire on which logs cease
to be thrown. Control of the tongue is, therefore,
indirectly, a stern discipline and mortification of all the
vices, especially those which are contrary to Charity.

As has been said so often the first tendency of every
faculty we have from nature is egocentric by reason
of the Fall. This tendency of course is to a certain
extent remedied by grace—but it remains all the same.
Egocentrism is another word for concupiscence taken
in its universal sense. To bring a faculty into order and
to direct its activity towards God—or in other words,
to cause it to exercise its activity in accordance with
right order—it seems a law (the law of mortification
that weighs on us) that we must first practise absolute
renouncement in its regard. To exercise the faculty
of vision as God wants us to, we must first purify that
vision by rigidly denying it every useless satisfaction
it seeks after. So it is with the faculty of speech. It has
been given to us to express the truth of the natural
order which our minds should reflect, to set forth the
truth of the supernatural order of which our spirit
should be possessed, to promote social intercourse
amongst men, and to express the praise of God which
should be drawn from us at the contemplation of His
works in the natural and supernatural order. The tongue
is given to us to glorify God, but it tends to glorify
self. It must therefore be denied every gratification in
this direction. It is more unruly, more difficult to curb

than any of the other faculties—hence silence practised constantly, unremittingly, seems to be the only resource. " For," says St. Gregory, " a man given to talk will never make any great progress in virtue," and he has but repeated what has been said in a certain passage —" a talkative man shall miss his way upon earth".

The rigid practice of silence has an added advantage. As has been pointed out there is a close connection between speech and imagination. The starting of one involves to a great extent the starting of the other. The more the imagination is emptied of images which serve to flatter self, the more free it is to receive those which aid the mind to raise itself to God—the more open is it to receive images pertaining to things of the supernatural order. The principal source of the natural images having been dried up, the supernatural will readily take their place and give rise to holy thoughts in the mind.[11] And when the imagination has been filled and stored and is readily stirred by what is supernatural, it is these images of the order of grace that will suggest the matter for speech and will moreover illuminate and elevate the themes of the natural order that may be selected for conversation. The man that is trained and exercised in the way described will speak easily of divine things or will speak divinely of human things. His conversation will not be a stumbling block for himself and will be a source of enlightenment and edification for his hearers.

We are silent in order to be able to speak as we ought. For this silence that is inculcated is not dumbness.

[11] Other sources of natural images are our unmortified thoughts and unrestrained use of the senses.

It is the cutting off of activity in one direction, in order
to allow it freedom of development in another. The
mere negative abstention from words as such is not a
good—the dumb never speak and yet they are not
necessarily more silent than others. The Christian virtue
is the cutting off of intercourse with men in order to
converse more freely with God, or about God and the
things of God. Silence is not anti-social because when
trained in this converse with the Lord, we can speak
with greater effect and greater utility for our neighbours.

§5.   Silence Indispensable for Recollection.

Silence is not inaction, but a means to a higher form
of activity of our imagination and intellect : " It
imports," says St. Thomas, " not a cessation from act,
but a cessation from distracting disorder and from
disturbing images in the imaginative faculty." Therefore the mere yielding to a disordered and distracting
train of imaginings may be in itself considered to be
a rupture of silence, even when there is no expression
given them in speech. We can in effect violate the spirit
of silence by giving free reign to our thoughts, if these
turn upon common, trivial or dangerous objects. The
spirit of silence is also disturbed by impetuosity in our
movements or by undue eagerness in the accomplishment of work. It is injured, too, by an uncontrolled
use of the eyes leading to the infiltration of images of
all kinds into the imagination.

Considered in this way, silence is closely akin to
recollection. The mere material cessation from the
use of the tongue is not silence but simply the pre-

requisite disposition to it. To be silent is to be recollected. The effect of this recollection is that the soul having withdrawn its powers from without inwards, can fix them on God. The mind that is fixed on God esteems all earthly and transient objects as valueless in comparison and despising them as refuse is not tempted to waste time in contemplating them.[12] *This state is at once the effect of and the condition needed for prayer. Silence is a necessary and indispensable means to prayer.* Prayer is nothing else than attention to God with a view to be instructed by Him, and to obtain His grace. If the mind of the pupil is intent and follows diligently the words of the Master, he can profit by the instruction given. The pupil is truly silent when his mind is fully alert to the matter taught and fully withdrawn from alien matters. On the other hand, if the pupil allows his mind to wander on topics foreign to the matter on hand even though he does not converse with those about him, he may be said to have violated the silence that the class demands. In the loud tumult of his wandering imaginations and of his wandering thoughts he is deaf to what is said. In this speechless violation of silence he does not heed the instruction addressed to him even though the sounds of the teacher's words fall on his ears. So it is with us and God : we must shut off the sounds of earth, in order that His voice may reach us. That is, we must gather in (the literal sense of the word, recollect) our exterior senses and our interior sensitive faculties, prevent them from straying after mere natural satisfaction and bring them under the control of the

---

[12] St. Paul, Phil. iii. 8. Our despising earthly things is given by St. Thomas as one of the signs that we are in the state of Grace. I. II. 112. 5.

will, operating through charity. This we must do if we wish to catch the voice of God. We cultivate silence in order to be able to speak with and to hear God easily.

Those who cultivate silence in the spiritual sense and who have acquired the habit of recollection are easily distinguished. They speak few words, but what they say carries extraordinary weight—even when the words have reference to the ordinary concerns of life. Their utterances do not flow without consideration. Their words, carrying all the force of the inner life of thoughts, are not uttered at random; neither are they mere flashes struck off the surface of the soul and varying with the nature of the sense impressions got from contact with external reality. They are not mere reactions to external stimuli. Recollected persons see straight and true and just, and a look of calm wisdom shines in their eyes. The balance of their judgment is not easily upset, " for an internal man quickly recollects himself, because he never pours forth his whole self upon outward things ".[13] This habit of reserve which is not the thing called secrecy, gives him power and influence over others—to whom he must always remain somewhat of a mystery. Given to internal converse with God, he never reveals himself wholly to creatures. Even in external activity, even in his very words, the silence is unbroken; for there is rupture of silence only when the interior attention flows out wholly into the exterior material occupation in which one is engaged : silence is lost if one loses oneself in one's work. Exterior occupations and the conversations with others which

[13] *Imit.* Book II. ch. 1.

they carry with them, would seem to make the observation of silence impossible. This is not so. It is quite possible to pass the greater part of the day in speaking, and yet maintain unbroken silence—provided a golden rule is observed. The rule is, never to speak merely for one's own sake or for one's own gratification, or to satisfy some impulse, but solely for the glory of God, for the right accomplishment of duty, for the promotion of truth, for the exercise of charity, for the comfort of the sorrowful and for the purpose of brightening the life of one's fellows.

One who aims at a truly interior life must cultivate a pure and simple soul that aims at reuniting in God all its interior powers and exterior occupations by recollection and retirement. "The spirit of God, which is pleased to dwell in a silent and peaceful heart, never comes into a soul that is in agitation or frequently troubled by the noise and disorder caused by its passions and strong feelings. It dwelleth not in a dissipated soul that loves to chatter idly and to communicate every passing thought in conversations that are the enemy of recollection."[14] "But in silence the devout soul goeth forward and learneth the secret of the Scriptures."[15] Our silence is perfect when we shall be talking constantly to God—and have ceased talking to men, for the mere pleasure to be found in such talk, irrespective of any good to be wrought by it.

Perfect and holy silence is animated conversation with God. Talking is, at least, in normal cases, the direct outcome of attention to persons and objects or both

[14] Bossuet.
[15] *Imit.* Bk. I. ch. xx. 6.

that are around about us. It is the surrender of our attention to, and our absorption in, external things or inward imaginings that have no bearing on the real good of life, that constitute the violation of the spirit of silence. For attention to, and interest in, things that cannot be referred in any way to God inhibit free intercourse with the Almighty. A person may talk a great deal and yet be silent, if silence be understood in the sense we have explained: silence is observed if our interest and attention do not stray from what is real. It is broken if activities of mind and imagination are wasted on what is unreal. St. Thomas spoke and dictated a great deal, yet he cannot be said to have violated silence in his life—for his words never proceeded from or were drawn from him by purely human or natural interests. Silence is meaningless unless it issues from or is intended to promote the control over our interior—control over our imagination and over our feelings.

The moment we allow anything outside, any external interest or object, to absorb our attention and distract that attention from that to which God desires us to attend, then we infringe silence. Silence is recollection as applied to the faculty of speech. It means the restriction of all unnecessary converse with men in order to allow our mind to converse more uninterruptedly with God. It makes prayer easy and is a safeguard which preserves devotion and spiritual sweetness from being dissipated. It makes the soul sensitive to the slightest whisper of the Holy Spirit. Recollection is absolutely necessary for the soul that aims at progress in the interior life. " Whoever," says the author of the *Imitation*, " aims at attaining to things internal and spiritual, must with Jesus, go aside from the crowd."[16] Whoever cultivates the spirit of silence acquires wisdom and attains to peace of heart. In the individual soul silence develops strength and power. In groups of persons joined together, whether naturally as in the family, or by vocation as in religion, where this spirit of silence is observed, fervour reigns, peace resides, all bitterness and uncharitableness disappear, and the works done are fruitful and blessed by God.

[16] Bk. I. ch. xx.

Printed in the United States
110653LV00005B/125/A